BRICK TOWER PRESS · GARDEN GUIDE

Gardening
in
Deer Country

for the Home and Garden

A Brick Tower Press Gardening Guide

Gardening
in
Deer Country

by Vincent Drzewucki Jr.

Interior Illustrations
Alison Gail

Cover Illustration
Lisa Adams

The Brick Tower Press ®
1230 Park Avenue, New York, NY 10128
Text Copyright © 1998
by Vincent Drzewucki Jr.
Interior Illustrations Copyright © 1998 by Brick Tower Press

Drzewucki Jr., Vincent
A Brick Tower Press Gardening Guide

.

Includes Index
ISBN 1-883283-09-4 softcover

Library of Congress Control
Number: 97-74018
Tenth Printing, February 2005

CONTENTS

USDA Hardiness Zone Map

TREES

SHRUBS

GROUND COVERS

VINES

PERENNIALS

ANNUALS/ BULBS

HERBS

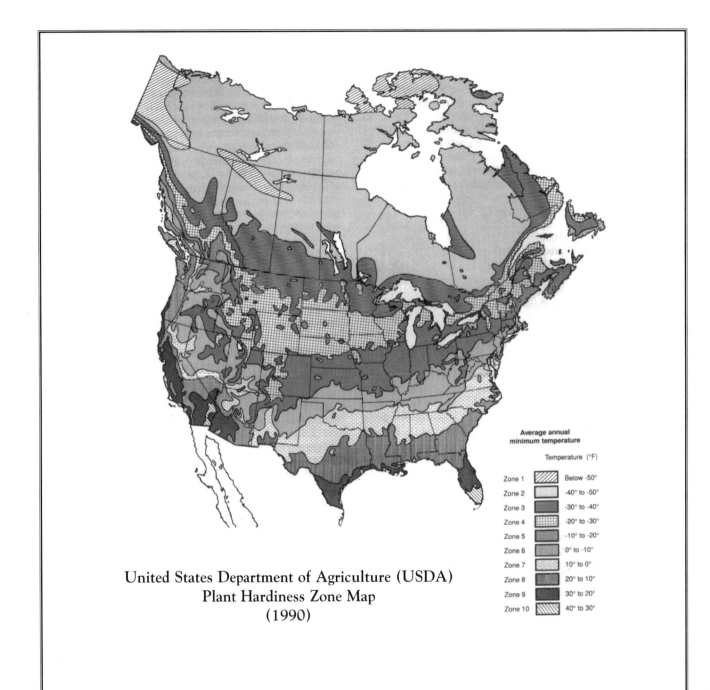

Average annual
minimum temperature

Temperature (°F)

Zone 1		Below -50°
Zone 2		-40° to -50°
Zone 3		-30° to -40°
Zone 4		-20° to -30°
Zone 5		-10° to -20°
Zone 6		0° to -10°
Zone 7		10° to 0°
Zone 8		20° to 10°
Zone 9		30° to 20°
Zone 10		40° to 30°

United States Department of Agriculture (USDA)
Plant Hardiness Zone Map
(1990)

THIEVES IN THE NIGHT

A family's dream come true–a new home on a modest plot of land, recently cleared and carved. A convenient location, several hundred yards from the main road and civilization; a small stream running through the back of the property. Compared to their previous home in a congested suburban community, the couple and their two children, the girl, 8, and her 5 year old brother, can enjoy a new home with pride in the schools, a crime-free community, a clean and healthy environment.

The country offers a large, outdoor lawn area for the kids to run and play and a beautiful landscape with room enough for a nice flower garden and perhaps a vegetable garden.

The family moved in. Shortly thereafter, a landscape contractor installed a luxurious green lawn and a tree for the front yard. The foundation planting and other plantings would become a family project over the next several months, fulfilling their dreams of creating a garden of their own.

The time had come. The family was all moved in. It was a beautiful spring morning and today was the day. Safely loaded into the minivan, the family headed to the local garden center. Selections were made: a few small shrubs, several rose bushes in bud and bloom, a dozen or so perennial flowers just beginning to bloom, and a few flats of colorful annual flowers. A shovel, a trowel, fertilizer, and other supplies necessary to complete the job rounded out the purchase. Loaded into the minivan with care, a day's worth of planting and family fun lay ahead!

The remainder of the day was spent planting. Everyone helped in whatever way they could. Mom directed most of the project, indicating exactly where each shrub and plant should go. Dad dug the holes for the shrubs and turned over the soil in the flower beds, all the while working in the right fertilizer and organic matter. The children helped too, and soon became especially skilled at carefully planting the delicate flowering annuals precisely where and how mom wanted. As daylight began to wane, the last of the planting was completed and mom and dad made sure the new additions were thoroughly watered. Entirely pleased with their accomplishments the family celebrated by dining out that evening.

Early the next morning disappointment and shock overcame the family. Mom was the first to discover it. While still in her bathrobe and slippers, she stepped outside into the cool spring morning air to enjoy the sweet fragrance of the newly planted roses and other flowers that would be there to greet her. But they were gone. The flowers and buds gone, as if someone had just clipped them off. They were nowhere to be found, they were just–gone. And so were the Columbine, Daylilies, and Hosta, right down to the ground, even some of the colorful annual flowers were missing and the hydrangea with the huge pink flowers, all

that was left were a few stubby twigs. Thieves in the night!

One by one the other members of the family came out and one by one the look of shock and disappointment overcame them. Where did they go? Who could have taken them? Thieves in the night?

Upon closer inspection, the evidence was clear. In the freshly dug soil, small prints appeared. But what marauding animal could have done this? Wild animals? Last night, on the way back from dinner, mom spotted the culprits along the main road. The tiny hoof prints?

Oh, DEER!

THE DEER FACTS

The previous story and similar ones really happen. The scenario occurs with ever increasing frequency. As the population shifts from congested suburban and urban areas to more rural areas, new home sites invade native deer habitats. More and more frequently garden and landscape professionals as well as wildlife experts are asked what can be done to reduce and eliminate damage to ornamental plants caused by white-tailed deer (*Odocoileus virginianus*).

The deer family in the US consists primarily of two species of *Odocoileus*, the white-tailed deer mentioned above which inhabits most of the US and the mule deer (*Odocoileus hemionus*) found west of the Mississippi River. Numerous subspecies of both exist. The primary, distinguishing characteristic to identify the mule deer is its large ears followed by their slightly larger size and weight. The deer family also includes caribou, elk, and moose, however the white-tailed deer are considered to be the greatest nuisance to the home gardener.

Not only does the homeowner and gardener suffer from deer damage, commercial enterprises suffer, too. Commercial

New York Asters, *Aster novi-belgi,* page 73

landscapes are prone to deer damage while it's estimated that hundreds of thousands of dollars, are lost each year due to deer browsing at nurseries producing trees, shrubs, and other ornamental plants. Other agricultural crops, fruits and vegetables, for example, incur damage as well. The purpose of this book, however, is to guide the homeowner in making the right choices of plants or alternative defenses that will eliminate or reduce deer damage in and around their gardens and home property.

The return of the white-tailed deer is by and large a paradoxical event. Their return, perhaps considered a miracle by some, is at the same time a growing cause of economic destruction. University studies by Cornell Cooperative Extension and other institutions show that deer populations are growing. Once reduced to a population of not more than 500,000 deer in the US around 1900, estimates today are that the white-tailed deer numbers may now exceed

15 million. Estimates show that in densely populated areas, 90 to 100 deer are not uncommon. The white-tailed deers' comeback is attributed to several factors such as restricted use of firearms and tougher hunting laws, diminished or nonexistent populations of natural predators, and conversion of abandoned agricultural lands back into deer friendly habitats.

Deer do damage by browsing, a pattern of feeding in which they select tender shoots, twigs, and leaves of ornamental plants, trees, and shrubs. Although deer are known to be finicky eaters, they are known to eat more than 500 different kinds of plants. Their taste can change and depends primarily on the season, nutritional needs, and the abundance or lack of abundance of their favorite foods. Be assured however that if and when times are bad and preferred foods are scarce, deer will eat just about anything.

On average, a healthy adult buck (male) or doe (female) needs to consume 5 to 10 pounds of food (4,000-6000 calories)

On average, a healthy adult buck (male) or doe (female) needs to consume 5 to 10 pounds of food (4,000-6000 calories) per day.

per day. Although this may not sound like a lot, just think how many tender new shoots, twigs and leaves it would take to satisfy a deer daily, and since deer often browse in groups of 2-7, that's a lot of ornamental garden plants. New plantings and well fertilized and maintained gardens are especially preferred by deer, and since deer are creatures of habit, once a new feeding area is found to be to their liking, future damage is easily predictable.

Like other wild animals such as raccoons, squirrels, rabbits, and opossum to name a few, deer have learned to coexist with us in our suburban and rural areas, and deer have learned to adapt to the changes we have imported to their environment. In fact, many deer have lost their fear of us and have adjusted their feeding schedule to avoid us and our dogs. Deer venture into our gardens at dawn or dusk for an undisturbed, leisurely meal. The following section describes things we can do to prevent this from happening.

DEER DEFENSE

KEEPING DEER OUT OF THE GARDEN

The primary purpose of this book is to help gardeners plan a great garden or landscape that will be resistant to deer browsing. Over the years I have had many requests from clients and friends for information concerning deer browsing damage. Although many suggestions, solutions, and products have existed in the field of horticulture for controlling deer browsing, it seems to me the most logical and cost efficient way of preventing deer from making a meal of your garden is to plan it to be resistant, by using plants that deer simply don't like. In almost every situation deer tend to be very selective, making gluttons of themselves when they come across a favorite plant and, more often than not, leaving less appealing plants alone. So, as a result, I've come up with an extensive list of plants that are known to be least preferred by deer. I've rated them according to their relative resistance and have even provided some that you should absolutely avoid. Whether you're planning a new garden or landscape or just trying to renovate and convert an existing deer devastated garden or landscape to a deer resistant one, I hope this list provides a guide for selecting the best plants to create a beautiful, deer-proof garden and landscape in deer country.

Before we get into selecting deer resistant plants, let's go through some of the standard method of deer defense methods that have been used and are available to reduce deer damage in gardens and landscapes that currently exist.

There are several ways to protect a garden and the surrounding property from deer browsing damage. Some are long term while others are very temporary. Most commonly used methods are fencing, chemical repellents including organics, electronic sound devices, dogs, and of course, using deer resistant plants. Each has its own unique advantages and disadvantages. Each may be used by itself or together to attain an effective combination.

FENCES

The fence provides perhaps the best means of protection against deer damage. As a physical barrier, a fence is somewhat permanent. To keep deer out it must be at least 8 feet tall, anything lower may act as a deterrent for some time; however, deer can using a fence rather costly. Also, a fence is usually highly visible and can detract from the aesthetic beauty of the garden and property. In certain situations a fence may be an economical and ideal choice especially when used to enclose and protect vegetable gardens, cut flower gardens, and other specialty plantings that need protection. Electric fences also provide an effective alternative. They're not as costly as other physical, barrier fences, but they do require periodic maintenance and may need to be replaced more frequently.

Rather than going through the expense of building a substantial fence, a simple and less costly method may prove effective at keeping deer out. Install posts around the vegetable or flower garden and run a few lines of heavy gauge fishing line, 50 lbs. test or more. The deer run into the line, dislike it and go no further. This creates an almost invisible barrier and leaves the garden untouched by deer.

Oddly enough however, some gardeners have had success using wire mesh, like chicken wire, or plastic netting, the kind used to protect fruit trees and berries from bird damage. The wire mesh or netting

Rose Mallow, *Hibiscus moscheutos,* page 78

usually easily jump any fence less than 8 feet if they need to. Care must also be taken to sink the fencing mesh or woven wire into the ground 18-24 inches deep since deer have been known to crawl under loosely constructed fences. The initial cost, especially on a large piece of land, plus the fact that a fence may need periodic maintenance or total replacement in 20-30 years makes is laid horizontally on the ground surrounding the garden. It seems deer don't like the feel of walking on it and apparently don't like getting their legs tangled in it.

For more extensive and detailed information on constructing fences for protection from deer contact your local Cooperative Extension office. (See page 102)

REPELLENTS

There are several repellents on the market that are effective. Most are organic chemicals that act as an odorous barrier while others repel by giving the plants a disagreeable taste to the deer. There are even now electronic audio devices now available that repel by sound. All provide an invisible, although temporary or seasonal means of control. Most are effective when repeatedly applied every 2-4 weeks, according to label directions, while others must be applied after every rainfall or after using sprinklers. In part, the repellents act to modify or control the behavior of deer,

Garden Petunia, *Petunia x hybrida,* page 90

allowing them to habitually avoid certain areas while learning to find dependable browsing areas elsewhere.

Most repellents that are based on odors that deer don't like are the most common. Deer find them either unpleasant or disturbing because they resemble the scent of a predator or danger. Odorous repellents are available commercially in garden centers, hardware and farm stores, and through mail order catalogs. These products are often formulations of ammonium soaps and non-commercial ingredients such as deodorant soaps, human hair, coyote and bobcat urine, or tankage (agricultural by-products such as dried manure, blood, and other animal residues). When buying and using commercial repellents, make sure they are labeled for use on the plants you are trying to protect and be especially cautious around vegetables, fruits, and berries.

Repellents can be costly and time consuming to apply and often must be reapplied after rain. Certain repellents depend on certain temperature ranges to be effective and the choice of repellent may change seasonally. The effectiveness of repellents will depend primarily on the current availability of natural food sources, a deer's appetite, stage of development, the weather, and frequency of application.

Some Commercially Available Deer Repellents include Hinder Deer and Rabbit Repellent, Bye Deer-All Natural Deer Repellent, IntAgra Deer-Away, Big Game Repellent, Sudbury Detour Rabbit and Deer Repellent. Milorganite is one of the most effective deer repellents. The regular use of Milorganite on lawn areas and around flowers, trees, and shrubs in the garden and in containers and pots provides proven results. The benefits are twofold. Milorganite is one of the best organic lawn and garden fertilizers around. It's non-burning and is a 100% natural organic fertilizer. Its main purpose is to feed, keeping plants healthy and vigorously growing. An added benefit is that Milorganite is known to act as an excellent deer repellent when used liberally around the property as frequently as every 4-6 weeks. It's an all natural, organic fertilizer that's made from activated sewage sludge from the Milwaukee Sewage District,

Wisconsin, perhaps providing its deer repelling characteristic.

Dried blood meal is an agricultural by-product that offers some degree of protection from deer damage. Like Milorganite, dried blood meal is good for plants as an all natural, organic fertilizer–a source of nitrogen for plants (nitrogen promotes green growth in plants). For best results, dried blood meal should be mixed with water and sprayed on plants, but scattering dried blood meal in its dry form around the base of plants is second best although be sure to lightly wet it to activate its odorous effect. To prevent deer damage dried blood meal must be applied on a weekly basis and following rain.

Bars of deodorant soap hung on or near susceptible plants is usually effective within a range of three to four feet. Soap bars can be left in their original wrappers and hung with string or wire. Insert the string or wire through a hole, drilled into the bar's center. Make a small pouch by cutting old stockings, pantyhose, or mesh onion bags. As the bars work best when kept wet, leave the wrappers on to make the bars last longer. Most deodorant soaps work well but experiment with different brands.

Lifebuoy consistently produces the best results. Bars or pouches need to be hung 3-4 feet apart on branches or stakes placed in and around the garden area. Replace them as needed.

Human hair is an effective, odorous repellent. Collect human hair from barber shops (hair from beauty salons may not be as effective). Put a few handfuls of hair in the small pouches described above and place throughout the garden, 3-4 feet apart on branches or stakes. Replace the hair midway through the growing season to prolong their effectiveness.

Use the following formula as a homemade deer repellent: 6 spoiled eggs, 3 tablespoons of Thiram 75% (a mild fungicide) and 1 quart of water. Mix thoroughly, using an old blender, if possible. (Do not re-use the blender canister for anything intended for human or animal consumption). Then, add 1 to 3 gallons of water and mix thoroughly. Spray on plants. Repeat as needed especially after rain or snow.

ELECTRONIC SOUND DEVICES

Several companies promote electronic or audible (ultrasound) equipment used to

American Holly, *Ilex opaca,*
page 41

repel deer and other animals by using sound, unheard by humans. As this affects only a very specific area, depending on the landscape or garden design, the abundance of many plants and structures tends to limit their effectiveness creating gaps where deer and other animals may feed unaffected. To achieve adequate protection in outdoor areas, several units may need to be employed at a cost of $80 or more per unit. Plus, given the ever changing conditions of landscape and garden areas due to weather, growth, changing seasons, and other factors, these devices don't have much merit. I remain skeptical as to their practical application in the landscape and garden due to the lack of unbiased and valid research currently available on their use in these situations. Perhaps future developments and cost reductions will someday make these devices more feasible.

DOGS

A good size dog of the proper temperament will provide a simple and effective means of eliminating deer damage. The dog may be kept on a leash outdoors at night or may be free to roam within a fenced area. A combination of a dog and the use of a 5-7 foot fence certainly will be an extremely effective control, although maintenance and replacement costs for both dog and fence may need to be considered.

Colorado Spruce, *Picea pungens*, page 45

DEER RESISTANT PLANTS

What deer don't like.

Using plants that deer don't like to eat–deer resistant plants–may at first seem as if it is the most logical and effective means of deer-proofing your garden, however it is not an exact science. What may work well in one place may prove ineffective in others. Hungry deer will try eating anything!

As deer behavior varies from location to location depending primarily on the season, weather (snow cover), nutritional needs, and the abundance or lack of abundance of their favorite foods, it is difficult to determine hard, fast rules. Documented evidence remains scarce, however experimentation through guided trial and error will eventually lead to a deer-proof garden. Luckily, results from the trial and error of others is available here. Good planning and a little patience is all you'll need to have a deer-proof landscape and garden.

Native Plants

Perhaps at first, the most logical method of creating the deer-proof landscape and garden is to mimic nature. By observing and noting those native plants that deer leave alone in your area you'll be able to draw some conclusions. Experience shows that once a native plant is found to be immune to deer damage, closely related members of that plant's family usually prove to be resistant as well. For example, plants in the Ranunculus family (*Ranunculaceae*) include our native Buttercup and Marsh Marigold (Caltha) as well as many cultivated members such as Columbine, Delphinium, and Winter Aconite to mention just a few, all of which are resistant to deer damage. As a result, if you find a particular native plant is resistant to deer damage, identify it to determine what family it belongs to and select other members for trial in your landscape or garden. For help with identification, bring a sample to a horticulturist at a local garden center, cooperative extension office, or botanic garden.

Factors that determine resistance:

Toxicity

Toxicity is perhaps one of the most common reasons for deer to leave a particular plant and its family members unscathed in your landscape or garden. The above is a good example. Members of the Ranunculus family contain members that are very poisonous to deer and other grazing animals, thus leaving the plants untouched more often than not. Daffodils are another good example of plants that are left alone by deer and rodents (especially squirrels), but there is no need for alarm. In most cases, large quantities of foliage and other plant parts would have to be ingested to have a toxic reaction. A word of caution however: whenever considering a new plant, find out about its relative toxicity when handled as some plants may give off toxins. Take proper precautions such as wearing gloves and long sleeve shirts.

Aroma

Aromatic foliage is more often than not shunned by deer. In fact many of the commonly cultivated herbs used for cooking and preparing dishes as well as those used in aromatherapy and for other medicinal purposes, are resistant to deer damage. Often, these herbs primarily serve a threefold purpose in the landscape and garden: They are deer resistant. They have specific use such as a flavoring, fragrance, and medicine. They provide ornamental value as an added benefit. Examples of deer resistant plants with aromatic foliage include Basil, Lavender, Thyme, and Yarrow.

Fuzzy Foliage

There is perhaps nothing more disagreeable to deer than a mouthful of fuzz. Deer just seem to steer clear of foliage that have a pubescent covering. The short, soft hairs that cover the leaves of certain plants such as Lamb's Ears, Dead Nettle, Rose Campion, and Black-Eyed Susan provide the plant with a characteristic that make them shunned by deer. It is safe to say that most other plants with fuzz covered leaves will provide resistance.

Lamb's Ears, *Stachys byzantina*, page 83

Prickly Parts

Thorns, spines, and needles provide good clues when determining a plant's resistance to deer damage. Hard, needle-type foliage found on many evergreens such as Spruce, Pine, and Juniper provide very good protection from deer damage. Also, thorny stems and branches of Barberry, English Hawthorn, and Japanese Flowering Quince provide additional protection. Deer will also avoid the hard, prickly edged leaves of American and English Holly and Leucothoe as well as Oregon Grape Holly. However, deer have been known to be carefully selective about consuming the soft, succulent buds and flowers from plants such as Rose and Hawthorn, while leaving the thorny covered stems and branches alone. Perhaps the additional protection provided by plastic netting or a fence or a trellis would be best.

MAKING THE RIGHT SELECTIONS

The remainder of this book provides a guide for choosing the right plants. The lists offer a resistance rating for each plant, however the rating is not hard and fast as it is only intended to be used as a guide. The ratings were determined through formal and not so formal research.

Remember, a plant's resistance may vary due to location, weather, season, environmental factors, and a deer's stage of physical development. Concentrate on using the plants deer have been known to dislike.

There are many plants that deer will leave alone. New landscapes and gardens, with a little extra work, can be designed and planned to use only those plants known to be deer-proof. For those whose landscapes and gardens already exist, perhaps a transition period makes sense. Add deer-proof plants while removing their favorites, employing the use of repellents as needed to prevent devastation.

Choose plants best suited for their location based on the amount of sunlight, soil, and water.

Besides being deer-proof, the plants

Black-Eyed Susan,
Rudbeckia maxima, page 82

chosen must be right for the area they are to be planted in. Be sure to consider how much sun the spot gets during the entire day. Consider whether the area is primarily exposed to full sun (direct sun all day), deep shade (no direct sun at all), or partial shade and sun (morning, mid, or late afternoon sun only, etc.). Also, consider the type of soil that exists in the area. Is it dominantly sandy, clay, or loam? Does the area drain well or do puddles of water persist or does the area stay soggy wet for extended periods, a day or more? Will the area be irrigated or will these plants need to depend on natural rainfall only? All are important considerations when selecting plants that will grow and thrive.

Choose plants that work well together–flower and foliage color, texture and size.

Finally, choose plants that will look good together. Like choosing what you wear every day, colors, textures, and proper fit or size are combined for a pleasing effect. Consider not only flower color when choosing a flowering plant, but keep in mind foliage color as well. Plants provide variations in texture, too. For example, large or pointed leaves provide a coarse look while many tiny, rounded, or smooth edged, small, fine leaves provide softer textures. Last, but not least, choose the right size plant for the area. Always consider a plant's mature height whether selecting shade trees or plants for a flower border. Generally, use larger plants in the background while shorter, low growing plants are best used up in front and as edging. The overall goal is to create harmony–combinations of colors, textures, and sizes that look good together.

Draw a plan first.

Draw a plan of the planting area first. For most projects, especially smaller ones, a rough sketch is all you'll need. For simple projects begin with paper and a pencil and a good eraser. Draw the area the way it exists now including buildings and permanent structures such as walks, fences, and driveways. Then using the pencil and eraser, add and subtract trees and shrubs using circular symbols, and mark small plants with an "X." Structures can be added or taken out using the pencil and eraser. The use of overlays drawn on transparent or tracing paper will allow you to create several designs, enabling you to choose the best one. Just draw what exists first, then overlay the transparent or tracing paper and draw in the new design.

Keep relative size relationships as accurate as possible. Using a ruler or scale will help with size relationships. Perhaps 1 inch on your paper could be equal to 12 inches or one foot of actual area. Better yet, use graph paper instead and let each square be equal to 12 inches or one foot. Experiment on paper, developing several alternatives. Always remember it is much easier to change a design or placement of a plant or structure on paper with an eraser than it is to change that same design in the actual landscape or garden with a shovel.

For big jobs it pays to hire a professional landscape designer. The cost of a good plan created by a professional designer is worth every penny in the long run. A good landscape designer will survey the area and create a design that will work best, taking into consideration all factors like existing sunlight exposures, soils, drainage, existing structures, and proper plant selection.

PLANTING TIPS

To achieve success, besides choosing the right plant for the spot,

Periwinkle or Myrtle, *Vinca minor*, page 67

proper planting and care are important. Always make certain that the soil is properly prepared before planting, that all plants are planted at the proper depth, especially trees and shrubs, and water everything thoroughly, immediately after planting. Proper planting ensures strong, vigorous growth, an abundance of flower productivity in flowering plants, and increased disease and insect resistance. The use of an anti-transpirant spray such as Wilt-Pruf will greatly reduce transplant shock when it's applied immediately after planting.

Spring is traditionally the best time to do most major plantings, however research shows that trees, shrubs, vines, and perennials planted in the fall are better established and develop a larger, healthier root system before they experience their first summer. Fall plantings often are better prepared and better established to survive their first hot, dry summer. Most annual flowers and other bedding plants should be planted when all danger of frost at night is past, usually mid to late May. It's always a good idea to check with your local garden center or Cooperative Extension office for planting dates in your area.

Prior to planting and perhaps even before choosing plants, have a pH test done on the soil in the planting area. The pH test will determine how acidic or alkaline an existing soil is. Every plant has a desirable pH range. Once you know the pH of the soil you're working with then you can either choose plants that like the existing range or you can raise or lower the pH accordingly. Soil testing and advice about choosing the right plants for the pH or how to change and maintain the pH in your area can be obtained at any reputable local garden center or Cooperative Extension office.

Nasturtium, *Tropaeolum majus*, page 91

PLANTING AND CARE OF TREES, SHRUBS, VINES, AND PERENNIALS

Once the right plant has been determined for the selected spot, dig a hole twice as deep and wide as the size of the plant's existing root ball or container. Mix thoroughly into the soil that came out of the hole a generous quantity of organic matter like compost or peat moss. Use about one

shovelful of organic matter to three or four shovelsful of soil and a few handfuls of Milorganite, bone meal, or superphosphate. Back fill the hole about halfway with this mixture, keeping in mind that enough soil mixture must be in the hole so that when the plant is placed in the hole, the top of the root ball or top of the soil in the container it came in is level with the surrounding area. Planting too deep will cause soil to come in contact with bark at the base of the plant causing it to rot, and perhaps causing the untimely death of the plant. When in doubt plant a little too shallow–the plant will eventually compensate by growing its root deeper.

Remove plastic containers before placing the plant in the hole. Always gently handle the plant by the container or root ball, cradling it with your hands and arms. For larger trees and shrubs use a sling made of a large piece of burlap or an old blanket to gently lower these larger plants into the hole. Never drop it in and always try to avoid breaking or shattering the root ball. Balled and burlapped plants can be placed in the hole with the burlap left on them. If it's natural fiber burlap, it will decompose over time. If it's plastic or some kind of synthetic burlap, gently remove it after setting the plant in the hole. Cut and remove twines and cords, especially synthetic fiber ones. With natural fiber burlap, it is a good idea to loosen it on top and push it about halfway down the root ball. If it's left tightly tied, exposed, or near the surface it may choke the trunk over time or act as a wick when exposed to the drying effects of the wind and sun near the surface, thereby drying out the root ball below. Make certain there is no twine, cord, or burlap left tied around the trunk that will restrict or choke the trunk as the plant grows.

Now, back fill around the root ball with the remainder of the soil mix, tamping it firmly with your foot until it's level with the surrounding ground. Next, build a mound of soil mix about a foot or more out from the trunk, forming a catch basin for water and rain to collect above the root ball to eventually percolate down where it's most needed for the next few months.

Finally, water thoroughly. Water as needed when the soil dries, checking mois-ture levels several times per week for the first few months.

For additional protection, young, smooth barked trees like ornamental cherry, maple, beech, etc. should have their trunks wrapped with paper tree wrap material or burlap for the first few years too protect against sun scald and frost cracks. Wrapping should start at the first set of branches and go down to the ground. As the tree matures and the bark roughens with age, protective wrapping is no longer needed.

A 3-4 inch layer of a natural mulch like pine or cedar bark, wood chips, or pine needles helps to conserve soil moisture, keeping the soil cool and preventing weeds from growing. For trees, shrubs, and vines no additional fertilizer is needed for at least the first year as the naturally existing elements in the compost–Milorganite and bone meal–is enough.

After the first year, feed trees, shrubs, and vines at least once a year applying, Milorganite or a well balanced fertilizer like 5-10-5 or 10-10-10 in the late fall or early spring. Perennials will benefit from additional feedings starting in late March and every 4-6 weeks until early fall when feeding stops. Use Milorganite or a well balanced fertilizer like 5-10-5 or 10-10-10.

Be careful not to water new plantings frequently until they've had time to develop new roots. As the plants become more established over the years, watering will be needed less frequently and if the right plant has been selected for the conditions, properly planted and mulched, normal, natural rainfall should be sufficient.

PLANTING AND CARE OF ANNUALS AND GROUNDCOVERS

Annuals and groundcovers are usually planted in mass plantings that can include hundreds or even thousands of individual plants, many of the same variety. To plant annuals and groundcovers prepare a planting bed. About a week before planting, clear the area of debris, weeds, dead leaves, etc. Do a soil pH test and choose the right plants for the area or correct the pH prior to planting. Spread a 2 to 3-inch layer of organic matter like compost or peat moss over the area with lime, if needed, according to pH test results; then spread a good fertilizer like Milorganite, 5-10-5, or 10-10-10 over the entire bed at the label's recommended rate. Work the material into the soil, mixing it thoroughly to a depth of at least 6 to 8 inches. Turn the soil by hand with a spading fork or by using a roto-tiller. Break up any soil clods and level the area with a level headed rake or bow rake. Let it sit for about a week. Now you're ready to plant.

Using a trowel, transplanter, or dibble, make a hole large enough to accommodate the young seedling or transplant, gently tucking it into the hole and firmly pressing the soil down around the plant. Space the next hole far enough away for the next plant to develop. Follow the spacing guidelines on plant labels or refer to reference tables for ideal spacing. Repeat the process until the entire bed is covered. A thin 1 to 2-inch layer of mulch placed on top of the soil between the plants will help conserve moisture, keep soil temperatures cool and will prevent weeds and erosion. Water the bed thoroughly and check soil moisture daily, watering as needed when the soil dries. Annual bedding plants and groundcovers should be fertilized every 4 to 6 weeks throughout the spring, summer, and early fall by broadcasting into beds a good fertilizer like Milorganite, 5-10-5, or 10-10-10 following the product's instructions.

Pest Problems

As with any living thing, plants can develop health problems too. Insects, fungus, bacteria, and even viruses, as well as environmental and mechanical damage caused by man or nature can cause the plant's health to decline and can even lead to the ultimate death of the plant. In fact, declining health due to environmental factors, poor maintenance, or mechanical damage often leads to more serious insects, fungus, or bacterial problems. Weak plants are the most susceptible. Good health is the key to prevention. Healthy plants will not usually need treatments with pesticides, however sometimes an unexpected health problem does occur.

As with people, plant ailments should be identified and treated as soon as possible. All plants should be looked at frequently, weekly if possible. A leisurely daily stroll around the grounds can be both enjoyable and purposeful in maintaining plant health. Look at and examine everything. Do spot checks, periodically looking at the undersides of leaves and along the trunks and branches. The more familiar you become with recognizing plants in good health the easier it will be able to recognize when a plant is having a problem, even if you can't identify it specifically on the spot.

Anything suspicious such as the development of spots on the leaves, any discoloration or the loss of overall vigor, as well as the presence of insects or unusual bumps or growths may be signs of a problem. The first step is to properly identify the problem, its cause, and, of course, the cure. For this you may need the help and advice of experts. Bring samples to a horticulturist at your local garden center or cooperative

Common Peony, *Paeonia officinalis*, page 81

extension office. They'll be able to help or call a certified arborist or landscaper who specializes in controlling insect and disease problems. More often than not you've made large investments in time, money, and effort to plan out your garden and landscape. Don't let a simple problem get a foothold that could lead to great losses.

A Deer Good-Bye !

Always remember that one of the greatest things about gardening is that it's not an exact science. There's plenty of room for experimentation, improvement, and learning your own way of doing it. When in doubt, consult with experts. Horticulturists are always happy to help and share–it's their nature. Don't worry, have fun, enjoy the rewards and just do it!

Now I hope you're well on your way to having a beautiful deer-proof garden and landscape!

Vincent Drzewucki Jr.
1997

Ageratum or Flossflower, *Ageratum houstonianum*, page 86

PLANTS RESISTANT TO DEER BROWSING

The plants listed on the following pages have been found to be non-preferred, in varying degrees, by deer. This does not mean that deer will not feed on them. Next to each description is a deer attractiveness rating. If natural or other food sources are available or abundant, the higher ranking plants will probably be overlooked by deer. This rating is a guide not a guarantee! Every geographic region will have its share of finicky deer.

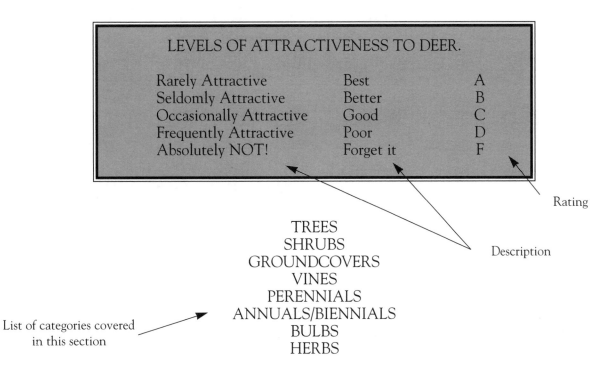

LEVELS OF ATTRACTIVENESS TO DEER.

Rarely Attractive	Best	A
Seldomly Attractive	Better	B
Occasionally Attractive	Good	C
Frequently Attractive	Poor	D
Absolutely NOT!	Forget it	F

Rating

Description

TREES
SHRUBS
GROUNDCOVERS
VINES
PERENNIALS
ANNUALS/BIENNIALS
BULBS
HERBS

List of categories covered in this section

Each category listed here has a detailed section starting with Trees on page 34. Not every plant in the list appears in the detail groupings but the ones detailed are more available to the home gardener. For further information please turn to page 102.

TREES:

LATIN NAME	COMMON NAME	RATING
Abies balsamea	Balsam Fir	F
Abies fraseri	Fraser Fir	D
Abies concolor	White Fir	C
Acer griseum	Paperbark Maple	C
Acer platanoides	Norway Maple	D
Acer rubrum	Red Maple	C
Acer saccharinum	Siver Maple	C
Acer saccharum	Sugar Maple	C
Aesculus hippocastanum	Common Horsechestnut	C
Betula papyrifera	Paper Birch (p34)	A
Carpinus betulus	European Hornbeam (p34)	A
Carya cordiformis	Bitternut Hickory (p35)	A
Castanea mollissima	Chinese Chestnut (p35)	A
Catalpa speciosa	Northern Catalpa (p36)	A
Cedrus atlantica	Atlas Cedar (p36)	A
Cercis canadensis	Redbud	D
Chamaecyparis obtusa	Hinoki Cypress (p37)	A
Cornus kousa	Kousa Dogwood (p37)	A
Crataegus oxycanthus	English Hawthorn (p38)	B
Cryptomeria japonica	Japanese Cedar	C
Fagus sylvatica	European Beech (p38)	B
Fraxinus pennsylvanica	Green Ash (p39)	A
Ginkgo biloba	Maidenhair Tree (p39)	A
Gleditsia triacanthos	Common Honeylocust (p40)	B
Ilex opaca	American Holly (p40)	A
Ilex pernyi	Pernyi Holly	B
Juniperus virginiana	Eastern Redcedar	C
Laburnum anagroides	Golden-Chain Tree (p41)	A
Larix decidua	European Larch	C

LATIN NAME	COMMON NAME	RATING
Liquidambar styraciflua	American Sweetgum (p41)	A
Magnolia x soulangiana	Saucer (and Star) Magnolia (p42)	A
Malus	Apples	D
Metasequoia glyptostroboides	Dawn Redwood	C
Oxydendrum arboreum	Sourwood (p42)	A
Picea abies	Norway Spruce (p43)	B
Picea glauca	White Spuce, (Alberta) (p43)	B
Picea pungens	Colorado Spruce (p44)	A
Pinus	Austrian, Pitch, Red, and Scots Pines	B
Pinus strobus	Eastern White Pine	C
Platanus occidentalis	Sycamore (p44)	A
Prunus avium	Sweet Cherry	C
Prunus serrulatai	Japanese Flowering Cherry (p45)	B
Prunus	Fruit-bearing Cherries, Peaches and Plums	D
Pseudotsuga menziesii	Dougas Fir	C
Pyrus calleryana 'Bradford'	Bradford Callery Pear	C
Quercus alba	White Oak	C
Quercus rubra	Northern Red Oak	C
Rhus typhinia	Staghorn Sumac	C
Robinia pseudoacia	Black Locust (p45)	A
Salix matsudana	Corkscrew Willow (p46)	B
Sassafras albidum	Sassafras (p46)	B
Sorbus aucuparia	European Mountain Ash	D
Thuja occidentalis	American Arborvitae	D
Tilia americana	Basswood	C
Tilia cordata 'Greenspire'	Greenspire Littleleaf Linden	C
Tsuga canadensis	Canadian Hemlock	C
Tsuga caroliniana	Carolina Hemlock	C

SHRUBS

LATIN NAME	COMMON NAME	RATING
Amelanchier arborea	Shadbush	C
Amelanchier laevis	Allegheny Serviceberry	C
Aucuba japonica	Goldust Plant (p47)	A
Berberis thunbergii	Japanese Barberry (p47)	A
Buddleia davidii	Butterfly Bush (p48)	A
Buxus sempervirens	Common Boxwood (p48)	A
Calycanthus floridus	Common Sweetshrub (p49)	B
Chaenomeles japonica	Japanese Flowering Quince (p49)	C
Cornus mas	Corneliancherry Dogwood	D
Cornus sericea	Red Osier Dogwood (p50)	B
Cotinus coggygria	Smoketree (p50)	C
Cotoneaster apiculata	Cranberry Cotoneaster (p51)	C
Cotoneaster horizontalis	Rockspray Cotoneaster	C
Cytisus	Scotch Broom	C
Daphne x burkwoodii	Daphne (p51)	C
Eleagnus angustifolia	Russion-Olive (p52)	A
Enkianthus campanulatus	Redvein Enkianthus (p52)	B
Euonymus alatus	Winged Euonymus	D
Euonymus fortunei	Wintercreeper	D
Forsythia x intermedia	Border Forsythia (p53)	B
Hamamelis virginiana	CommonWitchhazel (p53)	C
Hibiscus syriacus	Rose-of-Sharon (p54)	C
Hydrangea arborescens	Smooth Hydrangea	C
Hydrangea anomala subsp. petiolaris	Climbing Hydrangea	C
Hydrangea paniculata	Panicle Hydrangea	C
Hypericum prolificum	Shrubby Saint-John's-Wort	C
Ilex aquifolium	English Holly	C
Ilex cornuta	Chinese Holly (p54)	B
Ilex glabra	Inkberry (p55)	B

LATIN NAME	COMMON NAME	RATING
Ilex crenata	Japanese Holly	C
Juniperus chinensis	Chinese Junipers (p55)	B
Kalmia latifolia	Mountain Laurel (p56)	B
Kerria japonica	Japanese Kerria (p56)	B
Kolkwitzia amabilis	Beautybush (p57)	B
Leucothoe fontanesiana	Drooping Leucothoe (p57)	B
Ligustrum	Privet	C
Mahonia aquifolium	Oregon Grape Holly (p58)	B
Myrica pennsylvanica	Bayberry (p58)	B
Philadelphis coronarius	Sweet Mockorange (p59)	C
Pieris japonica	Japanese Andromedia (p59)	A
Pieris floribunda	Mountain Pieris	C
Pinus mugo	Swiss Mountain Pine (p60)	B
Potentilla fruticosa	Bush Cinquefoil	C
Pyracantha coccinea	Firethorn (p60)	C
Rhododendron	Deciduous Azaleas	C
Rhododendron spp.	Rhododendrons	D
Rhododendron spp.	Evergreen Azaleas	D
Rhododendron catawbiense	Catawba Rhododendron	D
Rhododendron carolinianum	Carolina Rhododendron	C
Rhododendron maximum	Rosebay Rhododendron	C
Rosa (x) hybrid	Hybrid Tea Rose	D
Rosa multiflora	Multiflora Rose	C
Rosa rugosa	Rugosa Rose	C
Salix	Willows	C
Skimmia japonica	Japanese Skimmia (p61)	B
Spiraea x bumalda	Anthony Waterer Spirea	B
Spiraea prunifolia	Bridalwreath Spirea	B
Symphoricarpos albus	Snowberry (p61)	B

LATIN NAME	COMMON NAME	RATING
Syringa persica	Persian Lilac (p62)	C
Syringa reticulata	Japanese Tree Lilac	C
Syringa villosa	Late Lilac	C
Taxus spp.	Yews	D
Taxus baccata	English Yew	D
Taxus cuspidata	Japanese Yew	D
Taxus (x) media	English/Japanese Hybrid Yew	D
Thuja plicata	Western Arborvitae	B
Viburnum carlessii	Koreanspice Viburnum (p62)	C
Viburnum x juddii	Judd Viburnum	C
Viburnum plicatum tomentosum	Doubefile Viburnum	C
Viburnum rhytidophyllum	Leatherleaf Viburnum	C
Weigela florida	Old-Fashioned Weigela	C

GROUNDCOVERS

LATIN NAME	COMMON NAME	RATING
Alchemilla	Lady's Mantle	A
Ajuga reptans	Bugle Weed (p63)	A
Arctostaphyllos uva-ursi	Bearberry (p63)	A
Asarum	Ginger	A
Bergenia	Bergenia	A
Cerastium	Snow-in-Summer	A
Convallaria majalis	Lily-of-the-Valley (p64)	A
Cotoneaster	Cotoneaster	C
Epimedium grandiflorum	Barrenwort (p64)	A
Ferns	Ferns	A
Galium	Sweet Woodruff	A
Juniperus	Juniper	B
Lamium maculatum	Dead Nettle (p65)	A
Pachysandra terminalis	Pachysandra (p65)	A
Potentilla	Potentilla	A
Pulmonaria	Lungwort	A
Santolina chamaecyparissus	Lavender-Cotton (p66)	A
Sedum	Sedum	A
Sempervirens tectorum	Hens-and-Chicks (p66)	A
Vinca minor	Periwinkle or Myrtle (p67)	A

VINES

LATIN NAME	COMMON NAME	RATING
Akebia quinata	Fiveleaf Akebia (p68)	A
Campsis radicans	Trumpet Vine(p68)	C
Celastrus scandens	Bittersweet (p69)	B
Clematis	Clematis	D
Euonymus	Wintercreeper	D
Hedera helix	English Ivy	D
Lonicera x heckrottii	Goldflame Honeysuckle	C
Parthenocissus tricuspdidata	Boston Ivy	C
Parthenocissus quinquefolia	Virginia Creeper	C
Polygonum aubertii	Silver Lace Vine (p69)	C
Vitis labrusca	Fox Grape Vine (p70)	A
Wisteria floribunda	Japanese Wisteria (p70)	B

PERENNIALS

LATIN NAME	COMMON NAME	RATING
Achillea millefolium	Yarrow (p71)	A
Aconitum carmichaelii	Monkshood (p71)	A
Alyssum	Perennial Alyssum	A
Anemone	Anemone	D
Aquilegia	Columbine	A

LATIN NAME	COMMON NAME	RATING
Arabis caucasica	Rock-Cress (p72)	A
Artemisia schmidtiana	Wormwood (p72)	A
Asclepias tuberosa	Butterfly Milkweed (p73)	A
Aster novi-belgi	New York Asters (p73)	A
Astilbe x arendsii	Hybrid Astilbe (p74)	A
Aubretia deltoidea	Purple Rock-cress (p74)	A
Aurinia saxatilis	Basket of Gold (p75)	A
Baptisia	False Indigo	B
Boltonia	Boltonia	A
Centaurea cineraria	Dusty Miller	C
Centranthus	Valerian	A
Chrysanthemum	Mums	D
Cimicifuga	Snakeroot	A
Coreopsis lanceolata	Lance Coreopsis (p75)	A
Delphinium elatum	Larkspur (p76)	A
Dicentra	Bleeding Heart	B
Digitalis	Foxglove	A
Echinacea purpurea	Purple Coneflower (p76)	A
Filipendula ulmaria	Meadowsweet (p77)	A
Gaillardia	Gaillardia	B
Geranium	Cranesbill (p77)	A
Geum	Geum	D
Gypsophila	Baby's Breath	B
Helenium autumnale	Sneezeweed (p78)	A
Helleborus	Hellebore	A
Hemerocallis	Daylily	D
Hesperis	Dame's Rocket	A
Hibiscus moscheutos	Rose Mallow (p78)	A
Hosta	Plantain Lily	C
Iris	Iris	B
Kniphofia	Red Hot Poker, Torch Lily	B

LATIN NAME	COMMON NAME	RATING
Linum	Flax	B
Lupinus	Lupine	B
Lychnis coronaria	Campion (p79)	A
Lysimachia clethroides	Japanese Loosestrife (p79)	A
Lythrum salicaria	Purple Loosestrife (p80)	A
Monarda didyma	Beebalm (p80)	A
Myosotis	Forget-Me-Not	B
Nepeta	Catmint, Catnip	A
Oenethera	Sundrops	B
Papaver	Poppy	B
Paeonia officinalis	Common Peony (p81)	A
Perovskia x hybrida	Russian Sage (p81)	A
Polemonium caeruleum	Jacob's Ladder (p82)	A
Primula	Primrose	B
Rudbeckia maxima	Black-Eyed Susan (p82)	A
Salvia	Meadowsage	A
Santolina	Lavender-cotton	A
Saponaria	Soapwort	A
Scabiosa	Scabious	B
Solidago hybrids	Goldenrod (p83)	A
Stachys byzantina	Lamb's Ears (p83)	A
Thalictrum	Meadow-Rue	A
Thermopsis	False Lupin	B
Thymus vulgaris	Common Thyme (p84)	A
Tiarella cordifolia	Foamflower (p84)	A
Trillium	Trillium	C
Veronica	Speedwell	A
Viola	Violets	D
Yucca filamentosa	Adam's Needle (p85)	A

ANNUALS

LATIN NAME	COMMON NAME	RATING
Ageratum houstonianum	Ageratum or Flossflower (p86)	B
Antirrhinum majus	Snapdragon (p86)	A
Arctotis	African Daisy	B
Begonia cucullata	Wax Begonia	C
Campanula	Canterbury Bells	B
Consolida	Larkspur	B
Dianthus	Sweet William	B
Helianthus	Sunflowers	C
Heliotropium arborescens	Heliotrope (p87)	B
Iberis umbellata	Candytuft	B
Impatiens	Impatiens	C
Ipomoea alba	Moonflower (p87)	A
Ipomoea purpurea	Morning Glory (p88)	A
Lobelia erinus	Lobelia (p88)	B
Lobularia maritima	Sweet Alyssum	C
Matthiola	Stocks	B
Mimulus cupreus	Monkey Flower (p89)	B
Mirabilis jalapa	Four O' Clocks (p89)	B
Papaver	Poppy	B
Pelargonium	Geranium	C
Petunia x hybrida	Garden Petunia (p90)	B
Salvia splendens	Scarlet Sage (p90)	B
Tagetes patula	French Marigold (p91)	A
Tithonia	Mexican Sunflower	B
Tropaeolum majus	Nasturtium (p91)	A

BIENNIALS

Digitalis	Foxglove	A
Myosotis alpestris	Forget-Me-Not	B

BULBS

LATIN NAME	COMMON NAME	RATING
Allium giganteum	Giant Ornamental Onion (p92)	A
Chionodoxa	Glory-of-the-Snow	A
Colchicum	Autumn Crocus	A
Crocus	Crocus	B
Eranthus	Winter Aconite	A
Fritilaria imperialis	Crown Imperial (p92)	A
Galanthus nivalis	Common Snowdrop (p93)	A
Leucojum	Snowflake	A
Muscari botryoides	Common Grape Hyacinth (p93)	A
Narcissus	Narcissus, Daffodils, and Jonquils (p94)	A
Puschinia	Striped Squill	A
Scilla siberica	Siberian Squill (p94)	A

HERBS

COMMON NAME	RATING	COMMON NAME	RATING
Angelica (p95)	A	Lavender (p96)	A
Anise (p100)	A	Lemon Balm (p97)	A
Artemisia	A	Lovage	A
Basil (p99)	A	Mullein	A
Borage Burnet	A	Oregano	B
Catmint (p99)	B	Parsley	B
Chamomile	B	Pennyroyal, European (p98)	A
Chives (p95)	A	Peppermint (p98)	A
Comfrey	A	Perilla	A
Dill	B	Rosemary	B
Fennel	B	Rue (p100)	A
Feverfew	A	Sage (p101)	A
Germander	A	Santolina	A
Horehound (p97)	A	Savory (p101)	A
Hyssop (p96)	A	Tansy	A
Lamb's Ears	A	Thyme	A

Betula papyrifera
PAPER BIRCH

ATTRACTIVENESS TO DEER: Rarely.
HABIT: Pyramidal when young, more irregular with age.
SIZE: 50-70'
LEAVES: Deciduous, 2–4" long, pointed oval with serrated edge.
FLOWERS: Inconspicuous.
TEXTURE: Medium.
CULTURE: Full sun, adapts well to a wide variety of slightly acidic soil types. A bleeder, do not prune in spring when sap is running.
LANDSCAPE/GARDEN VALUE: Good specimen tree for use in small groups. Very susceptible to two insect problems; birch leaf miner and bronze birch borer, all of which can be controlled.
Hardiness: Zone 2.
Native Habitat: Eastern North America.
Special Characteristics: Distinctive white bark. Golden yellow fall color. Young twigs and branches are reddish brown, similar to cherry. Often available multi-stemmed with three or more trunks.

Carpinus betulus
EUROPEAN HORNBEAM

ATTRACTIVENESS TO DEER: Rarely.
HABIT: Oval to round at maturity, pyramidal when young.
SIZE: 40-60' high and wide, known to reach more than 75'.
LEAVES: Deciduous, 2 1/2–5" long, oval, pointed tip. Double serrated edge.
FLOWERS: Inconspicuous, catkins.
TEXTURE: Medium in both summer and winter,
CULTURE: Full sun to light shade. Most types of soils, prefers well drained locations. Tolerates difficult conditions.
LANDSCAPE/GARDEN VALUE: Excellent specimen tree or can be planted in groups. One of the best small, low maintenance landscape trees. Can tolerate heavy pruning making it good for hedges, screens when sheared. Good for use in planters and near decks and patios.
HARDINESS: Zone 4.
NATIVE HABITAT: Europe.
SPECIAL CHARACTERISTICS: Superb winter interest, long, slender, and graceful branches emanate from a central main trunk. Attractive gray bark on mature fluted branches.

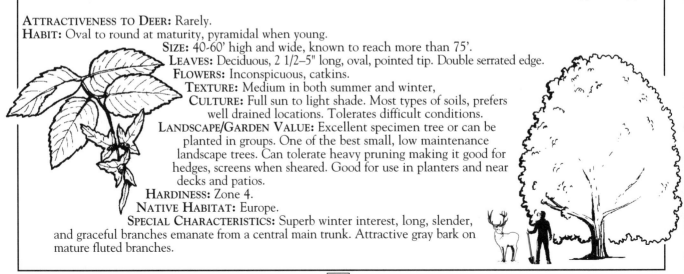

Carya cordiformis
BITTERNUT HICKORY

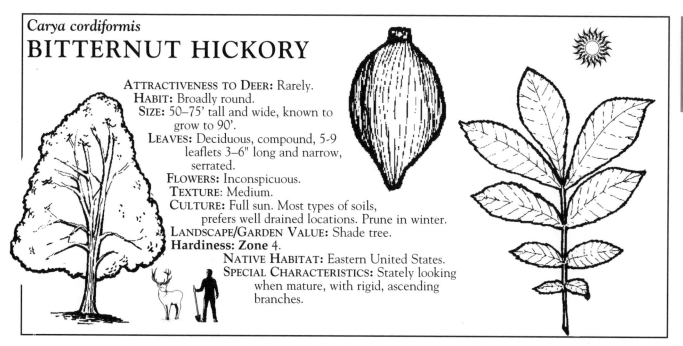

ATTRACTIVENESS TO DEER: Rarely.
HABIT: Broadly round.
SIZE: 50–75' tall and wide, known to grow to 90'.
LEAVES: Deciduous, compound, 5-9 leaflets 3–6" long and narrow, serrated.
FLOWERS: Inconspicuous.
TEXTURE: Medium.
CULTURE: Full sun. Most types of soils, prefers well drained locations. Prune in winter.
LANDSCAPE/GARDEN VALUE: Shade tree.
Hardiness: Zone 4.
NATIVE HABITAT: Eastern United States.
SPECIAL CHARACTERISTICS: Stately looking when mature, with rigid, ascending branches.

Castanea molissima
CHINESE CHESTNUT

ATTRACTIVENESS TO DEER: Rarely.
HABIT: Upright oval.
SIZE: 40–60' tall and wide, known to grow to 80'.
LEAVES: Deciduous, 6–8" long, 3" wide, coarsely serrated.
FLOWERS: Yellow to creamy white catkins 8" long.
TEXTURE: Medium.
CULTURE: Full sun, well drained, loam soil that is slightly acidic. Like pH range of 5.5–6.5. Good for hot, dry locations.
LANDSCAPE/GARDEN VALUE: Shade tree that produces nuts.
HARDINESS: Zone 4.
NATIVE HABITAT: Northern China.
SPECIAL CHARACTERISTICS: Produces valued edible nuts (chestnuts) that are enjoyed by man and wild animals.

Catalpa speciosa
NORTHERN CATALPA

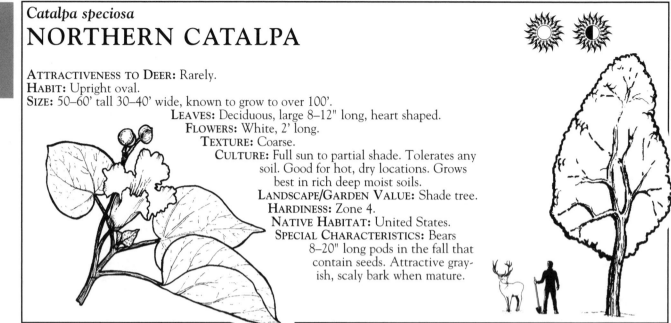

ATTRACTIVENESS TO DEER: Rarely.
HABIT: Upright oval.
SIZE: 50–60' tall 30–40' wide, known to grow to over 100'.
LEAVES: Deciduous, large 8–12" long, heart shaped.
FLOWERS: White, 2' long.
TEXTURE: Coarse.
CULTURE: Full sun to partial shade. Tolerates any soil. Good for hot, dry locations. Grows best in rich deep moist soils.
LANDSCAPE/GARDEN VALUE: Shade tree.
HARDINESS: Zone 4.
NATIVE HABITAT: United States.
SPECIAL CHARACTERISTICS: Bears 8–20" long pods in the fall that contain seeds. Attractive grayish, scaly bark when mature.

Cedrus atlantica
ATLAS CEDAR

ATTRACTIVENESS TO DEER: Rarely.
HABIT: Single or several erect trunks with spreading horizontal branches.
SIZE: 120' tall, 80–100' wide.
LEAVES: Evergreen, 3/4" long bluish or dark green needles.
FLOWERS: Inconspicuous cones.
TEXTURE: Medium
CULTURE: Full sun. Prefers well drained soils.
LANDSCAPE/GARDEN VALUE: Specimen tree, very picturesque with age. Provide plenty of room to grow.
HARDINESS: Zone 6.
NATIVE HABITAT: Northern Africa on the Atlas Mountains.
SPECIAL CHARACTERISTICS: Attractive silvery blue color. Produces 3" long, 2" wide cones, held upright on upperside of branches.

Chamaecyparis obtusa
HINOKI CYPRESS

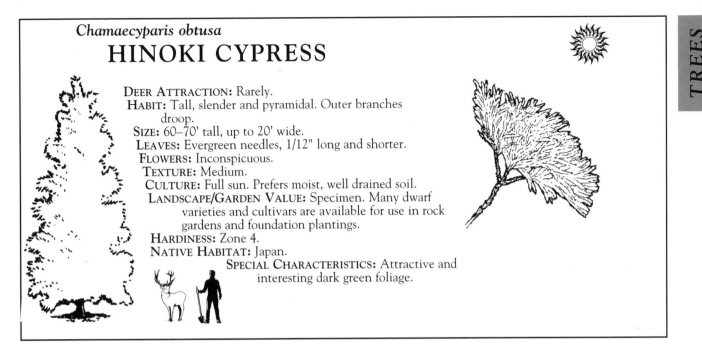

DEER ATTRACTION: Rarely.
HABIT: Tall, slender and pyramidal. Outer branches droop.
SIZE: 60–70' tall, up to 20' wide.
LEAVES: Evergreen needles, 1/12" long and shorter.
FLOWERS: Inconspicuous.
TEXTURE: Medium.
CULTURE: Full sun. Prefers moist, well drained soil.
LANDSCAPE/GARDEN VALUE: Specimen. Many dwarf varieties and cultivars are available for use in rock gardens and foundation plantings.
HARDINESS: Zone 4.
NATIVE HABITAT: Japan.
SPECIAL CHARACTERISTICS: Attractive and interesting dark green foliage.

Cornus kousa
KOUSA DOGWOOD

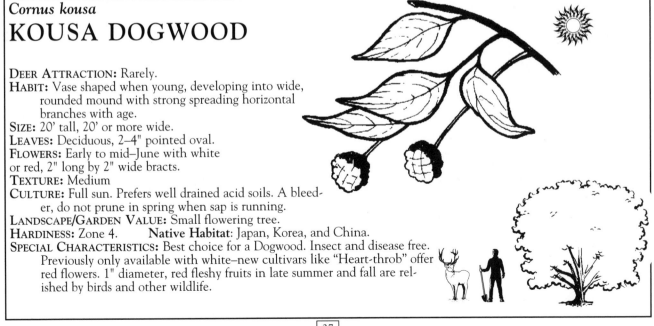

DEER ATTRACTION: Rarely.
HABIT: Vase shaped when young, developing into wide, rounded mound with strong spreading horizontal branches with age.
SIZE: 20' tall, 20' or more wide.
LEAVES: Deciduous, 2–4" pointed oval.
FLOWERS: Early to mid–June with white or red, 2" long by 2" wide bracts.
TEXTURE: Medium
CULTURE: Full sun. Prefers well drained acid soils. A bleeder, do not prune in spring when sap is running.
LANDSCAPE/GARDEN VALUE: Small flowering tree.
HARDINESS: Zone 4.   **Native Habitat**: Japan, Korea, and China.
SPECIAL CHARACTERISTICS: Best choice for a Dogwood. Insect and disease free. Previously only available with white–new cultivars like "Heart-throb" offer red flowers. 1" diameter, red fleshy fruits in late summer and fall are relished by birds and other wildlife.

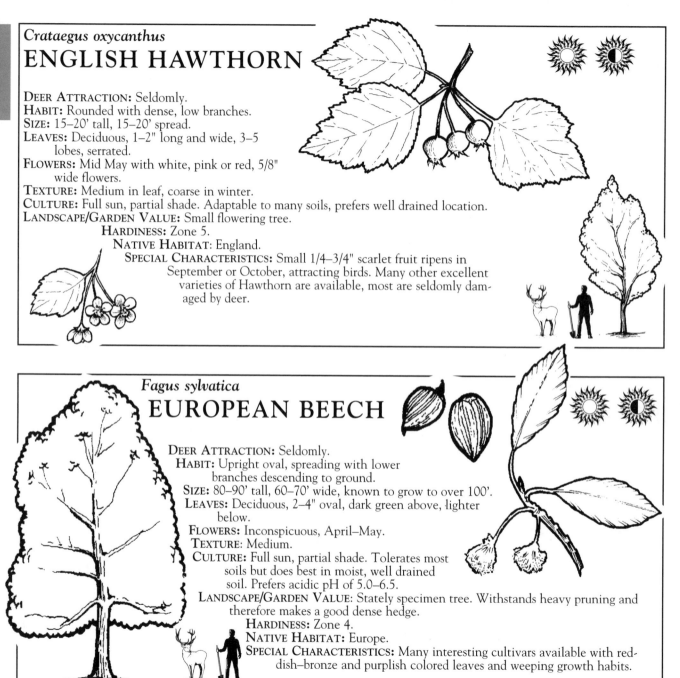

Crataegus oxycanthus

ENGLISH HAWTHORN

DEER ATTRACTION: Seldomly.
HABIT: Rounded with dense, low branches.
SIZE: 15–20' tall, 15–20' spread.
LEAVES: Deciduous, 1–2" long and wide, 3–5 lobes, serrated.
FLOWERS: Mid May with white, pink or red, 5/8" wide flowers.
TEXTURE: Medium in leaf, coarse in winter.
CULTURE: Full sun, partial shade. Adaptable to many soils, prefers well drained location.
LANDSCAPE/GARDEN VALUE: Small flowering tree.
HARDINESS: Zone 5.
NATIVE HABITAT: England.
SPECIAL CHARACTERISTICS: Small 1/4–3/4" scarlet fruit ripens in September or October, attracting birds. Many other excellent varieties of Hawthorn are available, most are seldomly damaged by deer.

Fagus sylvatica

EUROPEAN BEECH

DEER ATTRACTION: Seldomly.
HABIT: Upright oval, spreading with lower branches descending to ground.
SIZE: 80–90' tall, 60–70' wide, known to grow to over 100'.
LEAVES: Deciduous, 2–4" oval, dark green above, lighter below.
FLOWERS: Inconspicuous, April–May.
TEXTURE: Medium.
CULTURE: Full sun, partial shade. Tolerates most soils but does best in moist, well drained soil. Prefers acidic pH of 5.0–6.5.
LANDSCAPE/GARDEN VALUE: Stately specimen tree. Withstands heavy pruning and therefore makes a good dense hedge.
HARDINESS: Zone 4.
NATIVE HABITAT: Europe.
SPECIAL CHARACTERISTICS: Many interesting cultivars available with reddish–bronze and purplish colored leaves and weeping growth habits.

Fraxinus pennsylvanica
GREEN ASH

DEER ATTRACTION: Rarely.
HABIT: Upright spreading, pyramidal when young.
SIZE: 50–60' tall, 30–40' wide, known to grow to more than 80' tall.
LEAVES: Deciduous, compound, 5–9 leaflets, 2–5" long, 3" wide, tapered to a point at ends, finely serrated edges.
FLOWERS: Inconspicuous.
TEXTURE: Medium in leaf, very coarse in winter.
CULTURE: Full sun, tolerates most soils, prefers moist, well drained soils.
LANDSCAPE/GARDEN VALUE: Shade tree. Makes good street tree for curbside planting.
HARDINESS: Zone 3.
NATIVE HABITAT: Eastern North America.
SPECIAL CHARACTERISTICS: Fast grower, 3' or more per year under best conditions.

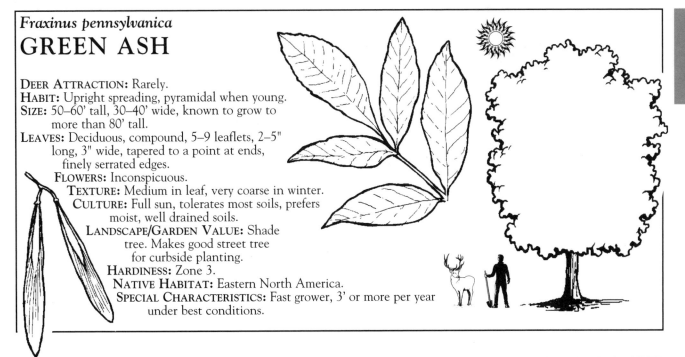

Ginkgo biloba
MAIDENHAIR TREE

DEER ATTRACTION: Rarely.
HABIT: Upright spreading, pyramidal when young.
SIZE: 80–100' tall, 50' wide or more.
LEAVES: Deciduous 2–3" wide.
FLOWERS: Inconspicuous.
TEXTURE: Medium in leaf, coarse in winter.
CULTURE: Full sun. Tolerates any soil, but prefers sandy, moist, well drained soils. Tolerates city conditions and air pollution.
LANDSCAPE/GARDEN VALUE: Shade tree.
HARDINESS: Zone 4.
NATIVE HABITAT: Eastern China.
SPECIAL CHARACTERISTICS: Very distinctive when mature. Plant only male, as females bear malodorous fruit when mature in 20–30 years.

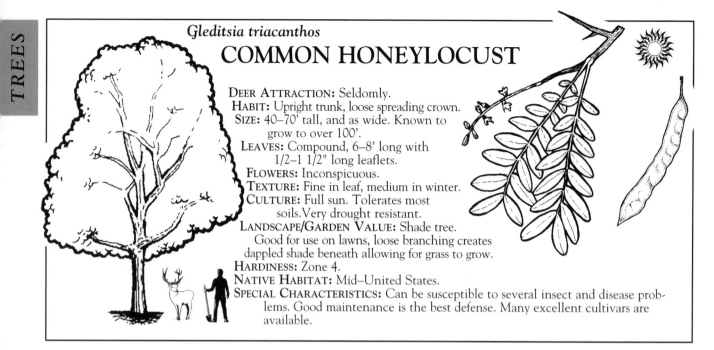

Gleditsia triacanthos

COMMON HONEYLOCUST

DEER ATTRACTION: Seldomly.
HABIT: Upright trunk, loose spreading crown.
SIZE: 40–70' tall, and as wide. Known to
  grow to over 100'.
LEAVES: Compound, 6–8' long with
  1/2–1 1/2" long leaflets.
FLOWERS: Inconspicuous.
TEXTURE: Fine in leaf, medium in winter.
CULTURE: Full sun. Tolerates most
  soils. Very drought resistant.
LANDSCAPE/GARDEN VALUE: Shade tree.
  Good for use on lawns, loose branching creates
  dappled shade beneath allowing for grass to grow.
HARDINESS: Zone 4.
NATIVE HABITAT: Mid–United States.
SPECIAL CHARACTERISTICS: Can be susceptible to several insect and disease prob-
  lems. Good maintenance is the best defense. Many excellent cultivars are
  available.

Ilex opaca

AMERICAN HOLLY

DEER ATTRACTION: Rarely.
HABIT: Upright oval, pyramidal when young.
SIZE: 40–70' tall, 20–40' wide.
LEAVES: Evergreen, 2–4" elongated oval with spines along edge.
FLOWERS: Inconspicuous.
TEXTURE: Coarse.
CULTURE: Full sun or partial shade. Prefers acidic, rich,
  moist, well drained soils. Will not tolerate drought
  conditions. Protect from drying winter wind and
  sun.
LANDSCAPE/GARDEN VALUE: Specimen tree.
HARDINESS: Zone 5.
NATIVE HABITAT: East Coast of United States.
SPECIAL CHARACTERISTICS: Female bears red berries
  in fall that attract birds. One male for every 2–3
  females in the area for berry production.

Laburnum anagroides
GOLDEN-CHAIN TREE

DEER ATTRACTION: Rarely.
HABIT: Upright with a rounded crown.
SIZE: 20' tall, 12–15' wide.
LEAVES: Deciduous, trifoliate with 3 or more elliptic leaflets, 2 1/2–3 1/2" long.
FLOWERS: Long 10–12" golden yellow clusters of 1 1/4" long pea-like flowers in late May to early June.
TEXTURE: Fine in leaf, coarse in winter.
CULTURE: Light shade. Prefers moist, well drained soil. Prune after flowering. Use in protected areas, out of direct winter wind and sun.
LANDSCAPE/GARDEN VALUE: Interesting small flowering tree. Use in shrub plantings and foundation plantings. Good for corners of house.
HARDINESS: Zone 5.
NATIVE HABITAT: Southern Europe.
SPECIAL CHARACTERISTICS: Bark is olive green. One of only a few small flowering trees that bloom in early summer.

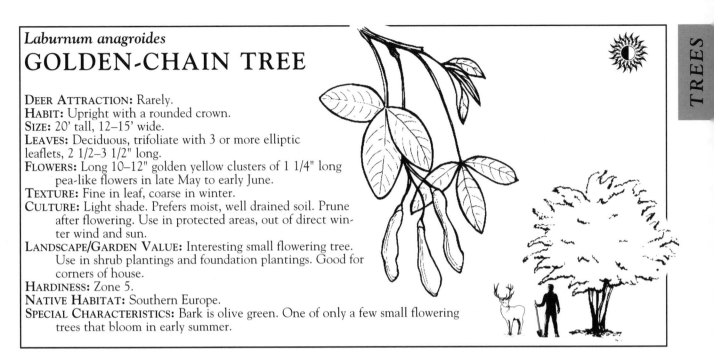

Liquidambar styraciflua
AMERICAN SWEETGUM

DEER ATTRACTION: Rarely.
HABIT: Upright rounded oblong crown, pyramidal when young.
SIZE: 70–80' tall, 50–60' wide. Known to grow to 120'.
LEAVES: Deciduous, 5–7" long and wide, 5 pointed lobes with serrated edge.
FLOWERS: Inconspicuous.
TEXTURE: Medium.
CULTURE: Full sun. Prefers rich, moist, slightly acidic soil.
LANDSCAPE/GARDEN VALUE: Shade tree.
HARDINESS: Zone 5.
NATIVE HABITAT: Eastern half of United States.
SPECIAL CHARACTERISTICS: Grows fast, 2–3' per year in best conditions. Attractive gray, deeply fissured bark. Fruit: 1–1 1/2" hard shelled capsule is messy and prickly in fall and winter.

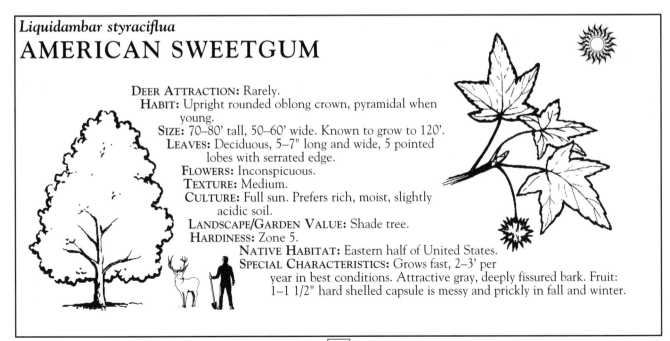

Magnolia x soulangiana
SAUCER MAGNOLIA

DEER ATTRACTION: Rarely.
HABIT: Low branched, rounded, spreading, large shrub or small tree.
SIZE: 20–30' tall and wide.
LEAVES: Deciduous 4–6" long, pointed oval.
FLOWERS: Large, 6–10" wide. Purplish outer edge fading to pink then white in center. Blooms mid to late April.
TEXTURE: Medium.
CULTURE: Full sun to partial shade. Prefers rich, moist acidic soil with a pH of 5.0–6.5. Prune after flowering.
LANDSCAPE/GARDEN VALUE: Small flowering tree. Use to soften corners of house.
HARDINESS: Zone 5.
SPECIAL CHARACTERISTICS: Very showy when in bloom. Heavy rains are known to knock petals off prematurely. Transplant balled and burlapped or from containers when young, best planted shallow.

Oxydendrum arboreum
SOURWOOD

DEER ATTRACTION: Rarely.
HABIT: Pyramidal with rounded top.
SIZE: 30–40' tall, 30–40' wide. Known to grow to over 75'.
LEAVES: Deciduous, 3–8" long, pointed oval.
FLOWERS: Numerous white, upright 4–10" long clusters of urn-shaped fragrant flowers, late June to early July.
TEXTURE: Medium.
CULTURE: Full sun or partial shade. Prefers moist, well drained acidic soil. pH 5.5–6.5.
LANDSCAPE/GARDEN VALUE: Specimen tree.
HARDINESS: Zone 4.
NATIVE HABITAT: Mid–Atlantic and Southeastern United States.
SPECIAL CHARACTERISTICS: Exceptional ornamental value all seasons. Excellent bright scarlet fall color. Slow grower, may reach 15' in as many years.

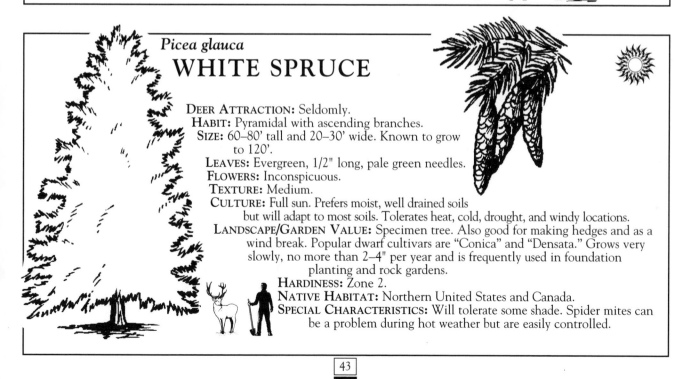

Picea abies
NORWAY SPRUCE

DEER ATTRACTION: Seldomly.
HABIT: Pyramidal with gracefully pendulous branches and branchlets.
SIZE: 60–80' tall and 40–50' wide. Known to grow to over 100'.
LEAVES: Evergreen, 1/2–1" long, dark green needles.
FLOWERS: Inconspicuous.
TEXTURE: Medium.
CULTURE: Full sun. Prefers moist, well drained soils but will adapt to most soils if provided with extra moisture during early development. Tolerates cold, windy locations.
LANDSCAPE/GARDEN VALUE: Specimen tree. Often used as a screen, windbreak, or hedge. Will tolerate close pruning when young to develop dense appearance. Prune in early spring. Avoid using in foundation planting and close to buildings.
HARDINESS: Zone 2.
NATIVE HABITAT: North and Central Europe.
SPECIAL CHARACTERISTICS: Many dwarf and weeping cultivars provide good shrub size specimens for rock gardens, shrub borders, and foundation plantings.

Picea glauca
WHITE SPRUCE

DEER ATTRACTION: Seldomly.
HABIT: Pyramidal with ascending branches.
SIZE: 60–80' tall and 20–30' wide. Known to grow to 120'.
LEAVES: Evergreen, 1/2" long, pale green needles.
FLOWERS: Inconspicuous.
TEXTURE: Medium.
CULTURE: Full sun. Prefers moist, well drained soils but will adapt to most soils. Tolerates heat, cold, drought, and windy locations.
LANDSCAPE/GARDEN VALUE: Specimen tree. Also good for making hedges and as a wind break. Popular dwarf cultivars are "Conica" and "Densata." Grows very slowly, no more than 2–4" per year and is frequently used in foundation planting and rock gardens.
HARDINESS: Zone 2.
NATIVE HABITAT: Northern United States and Canada.
SPECIAL CHARACTERISTICS: Will tolerate some shade. Spider mites can be a problem during hot weather but are easily controlled.

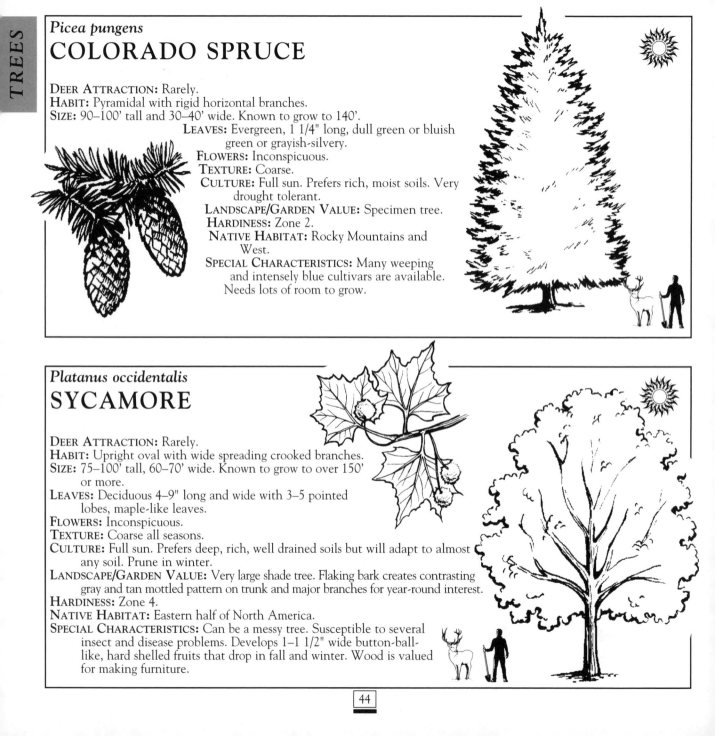

Picea pungens
COLORADO SPRUCE

DEER ATTRACTION: Rarely.
HABIT: Pyramidal with rigid horizontal branches.
SIZE: 90–100' tall and 30–40' wide. Known to grow to 140'.
LEAVES: Evergreen, 1 1/4" long, dull green or bluish green or grayish-silvery.
FLOWERS: Inconspicuous.
TEXTURE: Coarse.
CULTURE: Full sun. Prefers rich, moist soils. Very drought tolerant.
LANDSCAPE/GARDEN VALUE: Specimen tree.
HARDINESS: Zone 2.
NATIVE HABITAT: Rocky Mountains and West.
SPECIAL CHARACTERISTICS: Many weeping and intensely blue cultivars are available. Needs lots of room to grow.

Platanus occidentalis
SYCAMORE

DEER ATTRACTION: Rarely.
HABIT: Upright oval with wide spreading crooked branches.
SIZE: 75–100' tall, 60–70' wide. Known to grow to over 150' or more.
LEAVES: Deciduous 4–9" long and wide with 3–5 pointed lobes, maple-like leaves.
FLOWERS: Inconspicuous.
TEXTURE: Coarse all seasons.
CULTURE: Full sun. Prefers deep, rich, well drained soils but will adapt to almost any soil. Prune in winter.
LANDSCAPE/GARDEN VALUE: Very large shade tree. Flaking bark creates contrasting gray and tan mottled pattern on trunk and major branches for year-round interest.
HARDINESS: Zone 4.
NATIVE HABITAT: Eastern half of North America.
SPECIAL CHARACTERISTICS: Can be a messy tree. Susceptible to several insect and disease problems. Develops 1–1 1/2" wide button-ball-like, hard shelled fruits that drop in fall and winter. Wood is valued for making furniture.

Prunus serrulatai
JAPANESE FLOWERING CHERRY

DEER ATTRACTION: Seldomly.
HABIT: Vase-like upright.
SIZE: 20–25' tall and wide. Non-cultivars may grow to more than 75'.
LEAVES: Deciduous 2–4" long, 1–1 1/2" wide, pointed and slightly oval with serrated edge. New leaves emerge tinged red changing to green.
FLOWERS: Varies, white to pink, 1/2–2 1/2" wide, single or double. Flowers in late April through early May.
TEXTURE: Medium.
CULTURE: Full sun. Prefers rich, moist, well drained soil but will tolerate poorer dry soils.
LANDSCAPE/GARDEN VALUE: Excellent flowering specimen tree.
HARDINESS: Zone 5.
NATIVE HABITAT: Japan, China, Korea.
SPECIAL CHARACTERISTICS: Over 120 cultivars available for broad diversification of sizes, shapes, and flower types. Most popular cultivar is "Kwanzan" due to of its deep pink, double flowers. Grows to no more than 15–18' tall and 20' or more wide.

Robinia pseudoacia
BLACK LOCUST

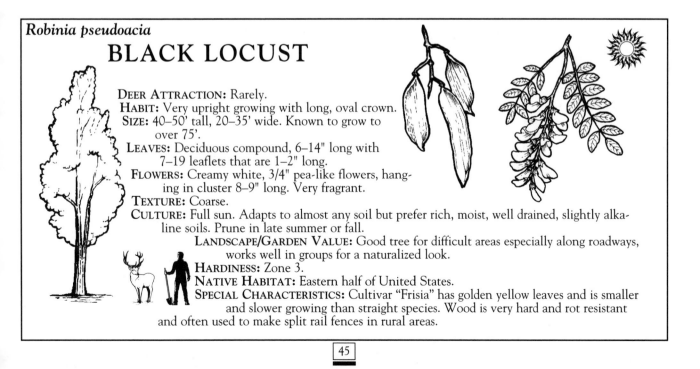

DEER ATTRACTION: Rarely.
HABIT: Very upright growing with long, oval crown.
SIZE: 40–50' tall, 20–35' wide. Known to grow to over 75'.
LEAVES: Deciduous compound, 6–14" long with 7–19 leaflets that are 1–2" long.
FLOWERS: Creamy white, 3/4" pea-like flowers, hanging in cluster 8–9" long. Very fragrant.
TEXTURE: Coarse.
CULTURE: Full sun. Adapts to almost any soil but prefer rich, moist, well drained, slightly alkaline soils. Prune in late summer or fall.
LANDSCAPE/GARDEN VALUE: Good tree for difficult areas especially along roadways, works well in groups for a naturalized look.
HARDINESS: Zone 3.
NATIVE HABITAT: Eastern half of United States.
SPECIAL CHARACTERISTICS: Cultivar "Frisia" has golden yellow leaves and is smaller and slower growing than straight species. Wood is very hard and rot resistant and often used to make split rail fences in rural areas.

Salix matsudana
CORKSCREW WILLOW

DEER ATTRACTION: Seldomly.
HABIT: Upright and spreading with contorted and twisted branches.
SIZE: 30' tall and wide.
LEAVES: Deciduous 3–4" long, 1/2–3/4" wide, tapered to a point, serrated edge.
FLOWERS: Inconspicuous.
TEXTURE: Coarse.
CULTURE: Full sun. Prefers rich, moist soils.
LANDSCAPE/GARDEN VALUE: Great small specimen tree. Although regarded by some as ugly looking, this is perhaps its real charm. Provides superb interest in the landscape with its contorted and twisting branches and weeping branchlets.
HARDINESS: Zone 4.
NATIVE HABITAT: China and Korea.
SPECIAL CHARACTERISTICS: A true oddity with merit. Other *Salix* varieties provide less distinctive but pleasing characteristics in the landscape.

Sassafras albidum
SASSAFRAS

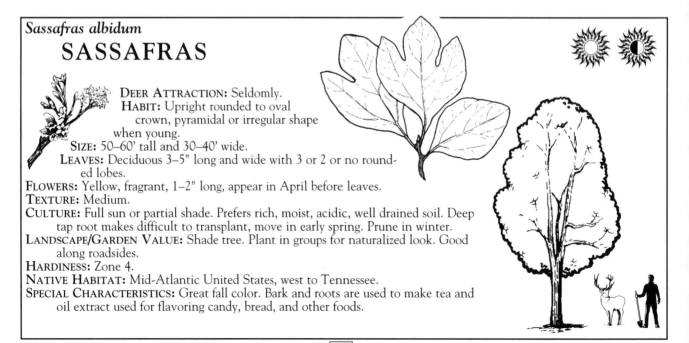

DEER ATTRACTION: Seldomly.
HABIT: Upright rounded to oval crown, pyramidal or irregular shape when young.
SIZE: 50–60' tall and 30–40' wide.
LEAVES: Deciduous 3–5" long and wide with 3 or 2 or no rounded lobes.
FLOWERS: Yellow, fragrant, 1–2" long, appear in April before leaves.
TEXTURE: Medium.
CULTURE: Full sun or partial shade. Prefers rich, moist, acidic, well drained soil. Deep tap root makes difficult to transplant, move in early spring. Prune in winter.
LANDSCAPE/GARDEN VALUE: Shade tree. Plant in groups for naturalized look. Good along roadsides.
HARDINESS: Zone 4.
NATIVE HABITAT: Mid-Atlantic United States, west to Tennessee.
SPECIAL CHARACTERISTICS: Great fall color. Bark and roots are used to make tea and oil extract used for flavoring candy, bread, and other foods.

Aucuba japonica
GOLDUST PLANT

DEER ATTRACTION: Rarely.
HABIT: Upright oval.
SIZE: 15' tall, 12-13' wide.
LEAVES: Evergreen, 6–7" long, pointed oval. Yellow variegated varieties are most common although all green and white variegated varieties are also available.
FLOWERS: Inconspicuous and dioecious, having male and female flowers on separate plants.
TEXTURE: Medium.
CULTURE: Partial shade, may burn in full sun. Adapts to most soils, prefers rich, moist, slightly acidic soils. Foliage is prone to winter damage from sun and wind–protect with anti-desiccant spray (Wilt-Pruf) in fall and winter.
LANDSCAPE/GARDEN VALUE: Foundation plantings. Interesting gold-yellow, spotted variegated foliage type is most commonly used in landscapes and gardens.
HARDINESS: Zone 7.
NATIVE HABITAT: Japan.
SPECIAL CHARACTERISTICS: Several varieties available, some with white variegation. Female plants produce red or yellow berries depending on variety. Sometimes grown indoors as a houseplant.

Berberis thunbergii
JAPANESE BARBERRY

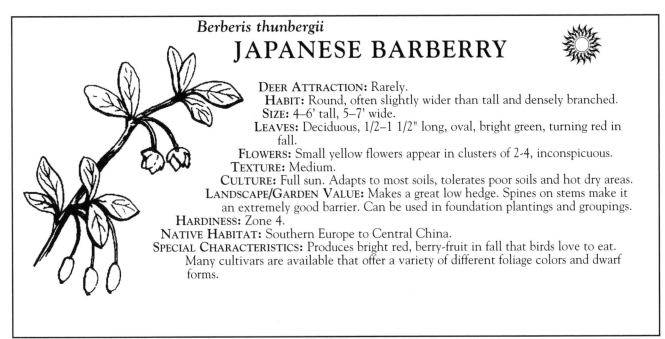

DEER ATTRACTION: Rarely.
HABIT: Round, often slightly wider than tall and densely branched.
SIZE: 4–6' tall, 5–7' wide.
LEAVES: Deciduous, 1/2–1 1/2" long, oval, bright green, turning red in fall.
FLOWERS: Small yellow flowers appear in clusters of 2-4, inconspicuous.
TEXTURE: Medium.
CULTURE: Full sun. Adapts to most soils, tolerates poor soils and hot dry areas.
LANDSCAPE/GARDEN VALUE: Makes a great low hedge. Spines on stems make it an extremely good barrier. Can be used in foundation plantings and groupings.
HARDINESS: Zone 4.
NATIVE HABITAT: Southern Europe to Central China.
SPECIAL CHARACTERISTICS: Produces bright red, berry-fruit in fall that birds love to eat. Many cultivars are available that offer a variety of different foliage colors and dwarf forms.

Buddleia davidii

BUTTERFLY BUSH

DEER ATTRACTION: Rarely.
HABIT: Upright and arching.
SIZE: Can grow to 15' tall and almost as wide.
LEAVES: Deciduous, 6–10" long, lance-like, dark green.
FLOWERS: Spikes that may be 8" or longer appear in August on current year's growth and continue until frost. Available in white, pink, purple, red and blue with an orange eye at center. Flowers are fragrant and attract butterflies like crazy!
TEXTURE: Coarse.

CULTURE: Full sun. Adapts to a wide range of soils, tolerating hot dry conditions. Prefers rich, moist, well drained soils. Often dies back down to the ground in winter, like a perennial. Cut back severely or to the ground in the fall or early spring to force vigorous new growth for flower production.
LANDSCAPE/GARDEN VALUE: Foundation planting or specimen. Mixes in well in mixed flower beds and borders, acting like a perennial. Its attractiveness to butterflies makes it a good focal point plant to create high interest and movement in an otherwise dreary area of the garden.
HARDINESS: Zone 5.
NATIVE HABITAT: China.
SPECIAL CHARACTERISTICS: Fragrance and its attractiveness to butterflies.

Buxus sempervirens

COMMON BOXWOOD

DEER ATTRACTION: Rarely.
HABIT: Round.
SIZE: 20–25' tall and wide.
LEAVES: Evergreen, 1/2–1 1/2" oblong oval. Shiny dark green on top, light green or yellowish green on undersides.
FLOWERS: Inconspicuous.
TEXTURE: Medium.
CULTURE: Full sun to part shade. Prefers cool moist soil. Protect from drying wind and sun in winter to prevent damage to leaves (use an anti-desiccant spray like Wilt-Pruf).
LANDSCAPE/GARDEN VALUE: Makes a good hedge and responds well to constant shearing for creating topiary and formal shapes. Good specimen plant.
HARDINESS: Zone 5.
NATIVE HABITAT: Southern Europe, North Africa, and Western Asia.
SPECIAL CHARACTERISTICS: Many cultivars are available that offer a variety of shapes, forms, and hardiness. Foliage has a distinctive malodorous fragrance that may be offensive to some individuals.

Calycanthus floridus
COMMON SWEETSHRUB

DEER ATTRACTION: Seldomly.
HABIT: Round and very dense.
SIZE: 6–9' tall and wide, can sometimes spread to 12' or more.
LEAVES: Deciduous, 3–5" long pointed oval.
FLOWERS: 2" dark red to reddish brown, very fragrant, appearing throughout mid-May, June, and July.
TEXTURE: Medium.
CULTURE: Full sun, but will tolerate shade as well. Prefers rich, moist soil but will adapt to poorer soils.
LANDSCAPE/GARDEN VALUE: Good foundation plant and mixed flower borders. Plant near or around decks , patios and other outdoor living areas to take advantage of its sweet strawberry-like fragrance when in bloom.
HARDINESS: Zone 4.
NATIVE HABITAT: Southeastern United States.
SPECIAL CHARACTERISTICS: Fragrant flowers appear in mid-summer.

Chaenomeles japonica
JAPANESE FLOWERING QUINCE

DEER ATTRACTION: Occasionally.
HABIT: Broad spreading, very dense with thorny branches.
SIZE: 3' tall, spreading to more than 3' wide.
LEAVES: Deciduous, 1–2" long oval.
FLOWERS: 1 1/2" wide, orange-red to deep red appearing in April.
TEXTURE: Medium.
CULTURE: Full sun to partial shade, blooms best in full sun. Adapts well to most types of soil and tolerates dry conditions.
LANDSCAPE/GARDEN VALUE: Foundation plantings and mixed flower borders.
HARDINESS: Zone 4.
NATIVE HABITAT: China.
SPECIAL CHARACTERISTICS: Develops small, 1 1/2" fragrant, green-yellow fruit in September and October. Often regarded as ratty looking by many, its thorny branches protect it from severe deer damage, and its flowers and fragrant fruits provide value in the deer resistant garden.

SHRUBS

Cornus sericea

RED OSIER DOGWOOD

DEER ATTRACTION: Seldomly.
HABIT: Round, broad and spreading.
SIZE: 7–9' tall, spreading to over 10' wide.
LEAVES: Deciduous, 2–5" long, pointed, oval.
FLOWERS: 1 1/2–2 1/2" wide, creamy white appear in late-June to early July.
TEXTURE: Medium.
CULTURE: Full sun to part shade. Adapts well to most soils, prefers deep, moist, rich soil. Does very well in poorly drained, wet, swampy conditions.
LANDSCAPE/GARDEN VALUE: Shrub borders and group plantings.
HARDINESS: Zone 2.
NATIVE HABITAT: Northeastern North America.
SPECIAL CHARACTERISTICS: Slender, upright stems are brilliant-red making this shrub quite attractive in winter especially against a snowy background. Also available is a yellow stem form "Flaviramea."

Cotinus coggygria

SMOKETREE

DEER ATTRACTION: Occasionally.
HABIT: Upright and spreading, loose, open habit.
SIZE: 12–15' tall and wide.
LEAVES: 1 1/4–3 1/4" long, rounded oval. Available in green and purple foliage.
FLOWERS: 6–8" long, loose panicles, yellowish green turning to smoky pink in June and July.
TEXTURE: Medium in leaf, coarse in winter.
CULTURE: Full sun. Adapts well to most soils, prefers well drained, rich soil. Tolerates dry and rocky locations. Needs extra care the first few years, especially water, but will eventually develop into a vigorous specimen that requires little attention.
LANDSCAPE/GARDEN VALUE: Shrub borders or group plantings. Can be used in foundation plantings but special consideration should be made for its eventual height and spread.
HARDINESS: Zone 4.
NATIVE HABITAT: Southern Europe to Central China and the Himalayas.
SPECIAL CHARACTERISTICS: Showy, smoky looking flowers and fruits.

Cotoneaster apiculata

CRANBERRY COTONEASTER

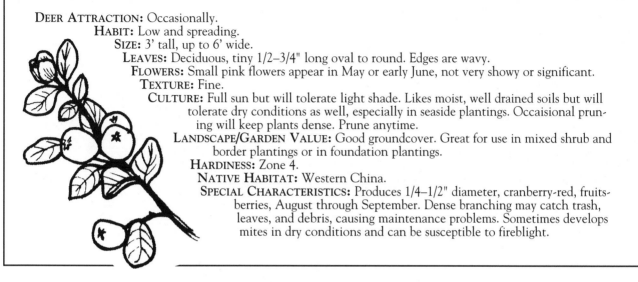

DEER ATTRACTION: Occasionally.

HABIT: Low and spreading.

SIZE: 3' tall, up to 6' wide.

LEAVES: Deciduous, tiny 1/2–3/4" long oval to round. Edges are wavy.

FLOWERS: Small pink flowers appear in May or early June, not very showy or significant.

TEXTURE: Fine.

CULTURE: Full sun but will tolerate light shade. Likes moist, well drained soils but will tolerate dry conditions as well, especially in seaside plantings. Occaisional pruning will keep plants dense. Prune anytime.

LANDSCAPE/GARDEN VALUE: Good groundcover. Great for use in mixed shrub and border plantings or in foundation plantings.

HARDINESS: Zone 4.

NATIVE HABITAT: Western China.

SPECIAL CHARACTERISTICS: Produces 1/4–1/2" diameter, cranberry-red, fruits-berries, August through September. Dense branching may catch trash, leaves, and debris, causing maintenance problems. Sometimes develops mites in dry conditions and can be susceptible to fireblight.

Daphne x burkwoodii

DAPHNE

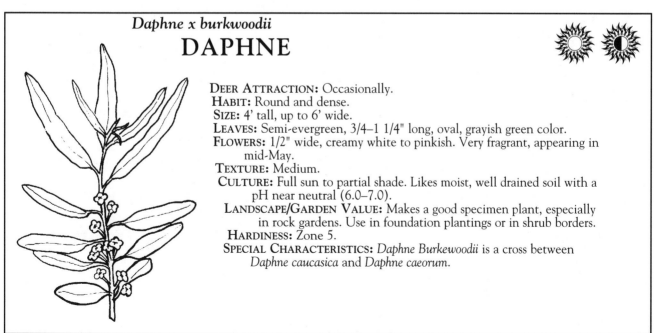

DEER ATTRACTION: Occasionally.

HABIT: Round and dense.

SIZE: 4' tall, up to 6' wide.

LEAVES: Semi-evergreen, 3/4–1 1/4" long, oval, grayish green color.

FLOWERS: 1/2" wide, creamy white to pinkish. Very fragrant, appearing in mid-May.

TEXTURE: Medium.

CULTURE: Full sun to partial shade. Likes moist, well drained soil with a pH near neutral (6.0–7.0).

LANDSCAPE/GARDEN VALUE: Makes a good specimen plant, especially in rock gardens. Use in foundation plantings or in shrub borders.

HARDINESS: Zone 5.

SPECIAL CHARACTERISTICS: *Daphne Burkewoodii* is a cross between *Daphne caucasica* and *Daphne caeorum*.

Eleagnus angustifolia
RUSSIAN-OLIVE

DEER ATTRACTION: Rarely.
HABIT: Round and spreading.
SIZE: 15–20' tall and wide, or more.
LEAVES: Deciduous, 1 1/2–3" long, lance like. Grayish-green color.
FLOWERS: Inconspicuous.
TEXTURE: Medium.
CULTURE: Full sun. Grows well in practically any soil. Prefers light sandy loam soils. Tolerates very harsh conditions and is good for seaside plantings, along roadways, and other dry areas. Occasional pruning will keep it looking dense and vigorous.
LANDSCAPE/GARDEN VALUE: Makes a good hedge or screen. Use in shrub borders and in foundation plantings where height is needed. Grayish color foliage is useful for lightening up areas and breaking up darker or all green group plantings.
HARDINESS: Zone 2.
NATIVE HABITAT: Southern Europe and Western Asia.
SPECIAL CHARACTERISTICS: Good salt and alkaline tolerance makes Russian-Olive an excellent shrub for seaside plantings. Develops crooked trunks and shedding bark.

Enkianthus campanulatus
REDVEIN ENKIANTHUS

DEER ATTRACTION: Seldomly.
HABIT: Upright and narrow growing shrub or small tree.
SIZE: 10–15' tall, known to grow to over 25'.
LEAVES: Deciduous, 1 1/2–3" long, pointed oval.
FLOWERS: 1/2" long, yellowish or light orange with red veins. Appear in May with new growth of leaves.
TEXTURE: Medium.
CULTURE: Full sun to partial shade. Prefers cool, acidic, rich, moist soil. (Same as rhododendrons).
LANDSCAPE/GARDEN VALUE: Great specimen plant. Mixes well with rhododendrons and azaleas. Flowers and excellent fall color makes it great for use around decks, patios, and other high traffic and interest areas in the landscape.
HARDINESS: Zone 4.
NATIVE HABITAT: Japan.
SPECIAL CHARACTERISTICS: Brilliant red and orange foliage in the fall.

Forsythia x intermedia
BORDER FORSYTHIA

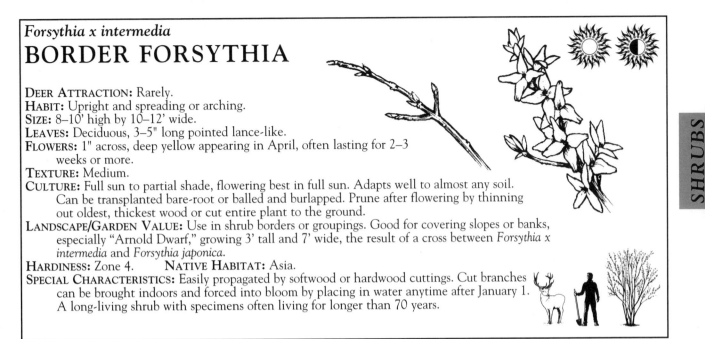

DEER ATTRACTION: Rarely.
HABIT: Upright and spreading or arching.
SIZE: 8–10' high by 10–12' wide.
LEAVES: Deciduous, 3–5" long pointed lance-like.
FLOWERS: 1" across, deep yellow appearing in April, often lasting for 2–3
　　weeks or more.
TEXTURE: Medium.
CULTURE: Full sun to partial shade, flowering best in full sun. Adapts well to almost any soil.
　　Can be transplanted bare-root or balled and burlapped. Prune after flowering by thinning
　　out oldest, thickest wood or cut entire plant to the ground.
LANDSCAPE/GARDEN VALUE: Use in shrub borders or groupings. Good for covering slopes or banks,
　　especially "Arnold Dwarf," growing 3' tall and 7' wide, the result of a cross between *Forsythia x
　　intermedia* and *Forsythia japonica.*
HARDINESS: Zone 4.　　**NATIVE HABITAT:** Asia.
SPECIAL CHARACTERISTICS: Easily propagated by softwood or hardwood cuttings. Cut branches
　　can be brought indoors and forced into bloom by placing in water anytime after January 1.
　　A long-living shrub with specimens often living for longer than 70 years.

Hamamelis virginiana
COMMON WITCHHAZEL

DEER ATTRACTION: Occasionally.
HABIT: Rounded, large shrub or small tree with contorted, spreading branches.
SIZE: 20–30' tall and wide.
LEAVES: Deciduous, 3–6" long, oval.
FLOWERS: 3/4–1" yellow and fragrant. Flowers can appear any time
　　between mid October through early December and can last up to
　　3 weeks or more.
TEXTURE: Coarse.
CULTURE: Full sun to partial shade. Prefers moist, rich soils and
　　will not tolerate dry conditions.
LANDSCAPE/GARDEN VALUE: Shrub borders or as a specimen.
HARDINESS: Zone 4.
NATIVE HABITAT: Eastern North America.
SPECIAL CHARACTERISTICS: Fragrant yellow flowers during
　　the absence of foliage add interest to the landscape or
　　garden in the fall.

Hibiscus syriacus
ROSE-OF-SHARON

DEER ATTRACTION: Occasionally.
HABIT: Upright and sightly spreading, large shrub or small tree.
SIZE: 10–12' tall, 8–10' wide.
LEAVES: Deciduous, 2–4" long with 3 lobes, edges coarsely toothed.
FLOWERS: 2–4" across, in various shades of red, white, purple, violet, and combinations, appearing July though August.
TEXTURE: Medium.
CULTURE: Full sun or partial shade. Prefers moist, well drained soil but will adapt to almost any except extremely wet or dry soil. Very easy to grow. Prune in early spring.
LANDSCAPE/GARDEN VALUE: Good for use as a specimen and in shrub borders and group plantings. Can also be used as a hedge or for screening. Avoid using close to walks, patios, decks, or other high foot traffic areas because of the mess and hazard from spent flowers.
HARDINESS: Zone 5.   **NATIVE HABITAT:** Asia.
SPECIAL CHARACTERISTICS: One of the most popular summer flowering shrubs. Easily propagated by softwood cuttings. Many good cultivars are available in numerous shades of flower colors and combinations.

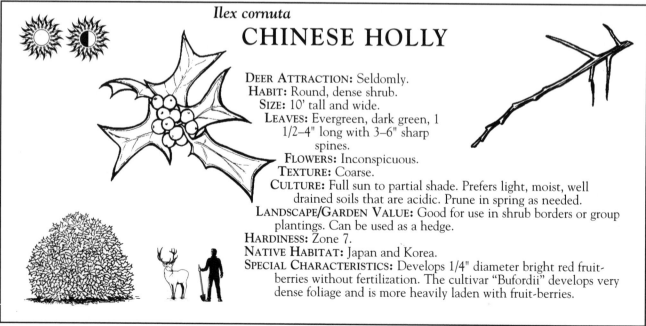

Ilex cornuta
CHINESE HOLLY

DEER ATTRACTION: Seldomly.
HABIT: Round, dense shrub.
SIZE: 10' tall and wide.
LEAVES: Evergreen, dark green, 1 1/2–4" long with 3–6" sharp spines.
FLOWERS: Inconspicuous.
TEXTURE: Coarse.
CULTURE: Full sun to partial shade. Prefers light, moist, well drained soils that are acidic. Prune in spring as needed.
LANDSCAPE/GARDEN VALUE: Good for use in shrub borders or group plantings. Can be used as a hedge.
HARDINESS: Zone 7.
NATIVE HABITAT: Japan and Korea.
SPECIAL CHARACTERISTICS: Develops 1/4" diameter bright red fruit-berries without fertilization. The cultivar "Bufordii" develops very dense foliage and is more heavily laden with fruit-berries.

Ilex glabra
INKBERRY

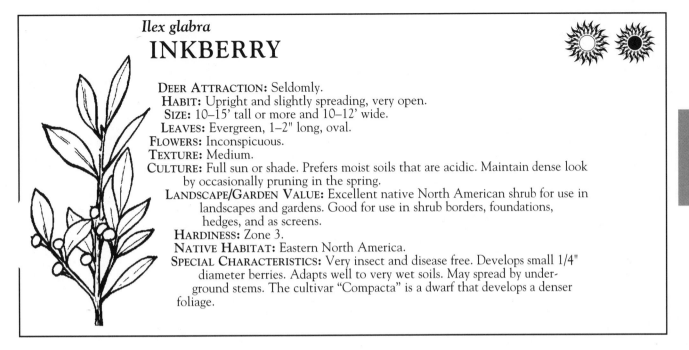

DEER ATTRACTION: Seldomly.
HABIT: Upright and slightly spreading, very open.
SIZE: 10–15' tall or more and 10–12' wide.
LEAVES: Evergreen, 1–2" long, oval.
FLOWERS: Inconspicuous.
TEXTURE: Medium.
CULTURE: Full sun or shade. Prefers moist soils that are acidic. Maintain dense look by occasionally pruning in the spring.
LANDSCAPE/GARDEN VALUE: Excellent native North American shrub for use in landscapes and gardens. Good for use in shrub borders, foundations, hedges, and as screens.
HARDINESS: Zone 3.
NATIVE HABITAT: Eastern North America.
SPECIAL CHARACTERISTICS: Very insect and disease free. Develops small 1/4" diameter berries. Adapts well to very wet soils. May spread by underground stems. The cultivar "Compacta" is a dwarf that develops a denser foliage.

Juniperus chinensis
CHINESE JUNIPERS

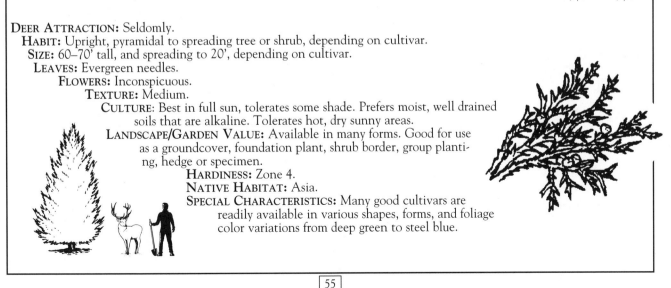

DEER ATTRACTION: Seldomly.
HABIT: Upright, pyramidal to spreading tree or shrub, depending on cultivar.
SIZE: 60–70' tall, and spreading to 20', depending on cultivar.
LEAVES: Evergreen needles.
FLOWERS: Inconspicuous.
TEXTURE: Medium.
CULTURE: Best in full sun, tolerates some shade. Prefers moist, well drained soils that are alkaline. Tolerates hot, dry sunny areas.
LANDSCAPE/GARDEN VALUE: Available in many forms. Good for use as a groundcover, foundation plant, shrub border, group planting, hedge or specimen.
HARDINESS: Zone 4.
NATIVE HABITAT: Asia.
SPECIAL CHARACTERISTICS: Many good cultivars are readily available in various shapes, forms, and foliage color variations from deep green to steel blue.

Kalmia latifolia
MOUNTAIN LAUREL

DEER ATTRACTION: Seldomly.
HABIT: Rounded, upright branched shrub.
SIZE: 7–10' or more in the wild.
LEAVES: Evergreen, 2–4" long pointed oval.
FLOWERS: 1" across. Colors vary from white to pink and deep rose with purple spotting in centers, appearing in early to mid-June.
TEXTURE: Medium.
CULTURE: Full sun to deep shade. Prefers acidic, cool, moist, well drained soil. Flowers best in sunny locations. Prune spent flowers immediately after they fade. Use an organic mulch to keep soil and roots cool and moist.
LANDSCAPE/GARDEN VALUE: Good for shady shrub borders, foundation, and group plantings.
HARDINESS: Zone 4.
NATIVE HABITAT: Eastern North America.
SPECIAL CHARACTERISTICS: Great native shrub. In old-age, Mountain Laurels become loose and straggly in branching habit with gnarled looking trunks and branches.

Kerria japonica
JAPANESE KERRIA

DEER ATTRACTION: Seldomly.
HABIT: Upright and arching.
SIZE: 4–6' tall, 6–9' wide.
LEAVES: Deciduous, 2" long, tapered with serrated edge.
FLOWERS: 1 1/2" across, bright yellow, appear in late April to early May and last for 2 weeks or more. May flower sporadically throughout the growing season.
TEXTURE: Fine.
CULTURE: Full sun. Prefers rich, well drained soil. Prune after flowering in the spring.
LANDSCAPE/GARDEN VALUE: Good for shrub borders and group plantings.
HARDINESS: Zone 4.
NATIVE HABITAT: China.
SPECIAL CHARACTERISTICS: A very vigorous grower often tolerating harsh conditions and neglect. Will sometimes continue blooming into June or later depending on the weather.

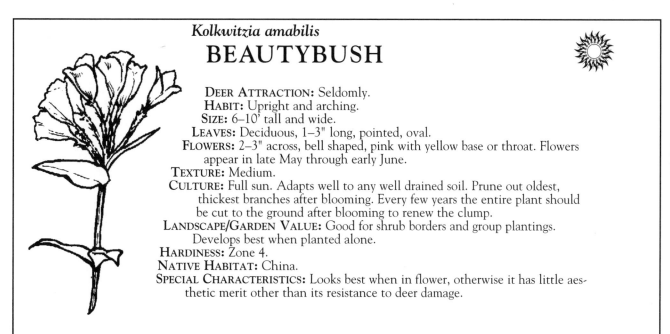

Kolkwitzia amabilis
BEAUTYBUSH

DEER ATTRACTION: Seldomly.
HABIT: Upright and arching.
SIZE: 6–10' tall and wide.
LEAVES: Deciduous, 1–3" long, pointed, oval.
FLOWERS: 2–3" across, bell shaped, pink with yellow base or throat. Flowers
    appear in late May through early June.
TEXTURE: Medium.
CULTURE: Full sun. Adapts well to any well drained soil. Prune out oldest,
    thickest branches after blooming. Every few years the entire plant should
    be cut to the ground after blooming to renew the clump.
LANDSCAPE/GARDEN VALUE: Good for shrub borders and group plantings.
    Develops best when planted alone.
HARDINESS: Zone 4.
NATIVE HABITAT: China.
SPECIAL CHARACTERISTICS: Looks best when in flower, otherwise it has little aes-
    thetic merit other than its resistance to deer damage.

Leucothoe fontanesiana
DROOPING LEUCOTHOE

DEER ATTRACTION: Seldomly.
HABIT: Low spreading and arching.
SIZE: 2–3' tall, 3–4' wide.
LEAVES: Evergreen, 2–5" long, pointed oval. Dark green and shiny.
    New growth color emerges bronze–red changing to dark green.
    Variegated varieties available.
FLOWERS: Fragrant, white, 1/4" long, hang in 2–3" long groups or sprays that appear
    beneath foliage.
TEXTURE: Medium.
CULTURE: Best in partial shade to full sun. Prefers acidic soils that are moist and well
    drained. Will not tolerate dry conditions. Avoid planting where drying winds and sun
    will cause damage. Protect with an anti-desiccant spray (Wilt-Pruf) where necessary.
LANDSCAPE/GARDEN VALUE: Good along front edge of shrub borders, group, and foundation plantings especially
    where shade dominates. Since Leucothoe is a shade loving, low growing and spreading shrub it is especially useful
    for placement under larger shrubs that have become leggy and sparse near the ground (around old
    Rhododendrons, Laurels, Japanese andromedia etc.).
HARDINESS: Zone 4.
NATIVE HABITAT: Virginia, Tennessee, and Georgia.

Mahonia aquifolium
OREGON GRAPE HOLLY

DEER ATTRACTION: Seldomly.
HABIT: Upright and somewhat spreading.
SIZE: 3–6' tall, or more, 3–5' wide spread.
LEAVES: Evergreen compound leaf with 5–9 leaflets that are 2–3" long, oval with spines along the edge. Leaves are dark green and shiny, often turning purple-bronze in winter. New growth emerges reddish in color.
FLOWERS: Slightly fragrant, small yellow flowers appear in April.
TEXTURE: Medium.
CULTURE: Prefers shade to full sun. Plant in acidic, moist, well drained soil. Avoid planting in sunny, hot, dry, windy areas. Protect with an anti-desiccant spray (Wilt-Pruf) where necessary.
LANDSCAPE/GARDEN VALUE: Good for shady shrub borders and foundation plantings.
HARDINESS: Zone 4.
NATIVE HABITAT: Pacific Northwest of United States through British Columbia, Canada.
SPECIAL CHARACTERISTICS: Develops blue-black berries, 1/3" diameter in August and September that may persist through December if birds and other wildlife don't get it first.

Myrica pennsylvanica
BAYBERRY

DEER ATTRACTION: Seldomly.
HABIT: Upright, rounded and dense.
SIZE: 6–9' tall and wide.
LEAVES: Deciduous, sometimes semi-evergreen. 1 1/2–4" long, oblong oval. Shiny green leaves are aromatic when crushed.
FLOWERS: Inconspicuous.
TEXTURE: Fine.
CULTURE: Full sun to partial shade. Thrives in poor, sandy and clay soils. Will tolerate seaside conditions and salt spray. Very adaptable.
LANDSCAPE/GARDEN VALUE: Use in shrub borders, group and foundation plantings. Makes a good hedge and screening plant. Adapts well to very poor conditions.
HARDINESS: Zone 2.
NATIVE HABITAT: East Coast of North America from Newfoundland to Maryland.
SPECIAL CHARACTERISTICS: Develops small, waxy, gray-black-purple, 1/6" fruits-berries that appear in September and can persist until April and are used to make bayberry candles. All parts are aromatic when crushed. Leaves do not turn color in fall and remain on plant late into fall and early winter or may persist and never fall off.

Philadelphis coronarius
SWEET MOCKORANGE

DEER ATTRACTION: Occasionally.
HABIT: Round shrub. Grows rather fast.
SIZE: 10' tall and wide.
LEAVES: Deciduous, green, 1 1/2–3" long and almost as wide, oval.
FLOWERS: Very fragrant, white, 1–2" wide. Blooms appear in late May or early June in groupings of 5–7 flowers each.
TEXTURE: Coarse.
CULTURE: Best in full sun or light shade. Prefers organically rich, moist, well drained soil. Flowers best on new, vigorous growth. Prune immediately after flowers fade by cutting out (down to the base) the oldest, thickest, wooded branches to encourage new growth.
LANDSCAPE/GARDEN VALUE: Use in shrub borders and mass plantings. Fragrant flowers make it great for use near and around decks and patios as well as along walks and paths or other high traffic areas.
HARDINESS: Zone 4.
NATIVE HABITAT: Europe.
SPECIAL CHARACTERISTICS: Has interesting orange-brown exfoliating bark.

Pieris japonica
JAPANESE ANDROMEDA

DEER ATTRACTION: Rarely.
HABIT: Densely upright and spreading.
SIZE: 6–8' tall and wide, known to grow to 12' or more.
LEAVES: Evergreen, 1 1/2–3" long, oblong, and pointed with a slightly serrated edge. Shiny dark green on top, light green beneath.
FLOWERS: Lightly fragrant, white, 1/5" long, bell-shaped flowers appear on 3–6" long clusters. Blooms mid to late March for several weeks.
TEXTURE: Medium.
CULTURE: Full sun or partial shade. Prefers moist, organically rich, well drained, acidic soil. Requires little or no pruning. Dead head flowers shortly after flowers fade. Susceptible to lace bug. Provide winter protection from drying wind and sun with an anti-desiccant spray (Wilt-Pruf etc.)
LANDSCAPE/GARDEN VALUE: Makes great flowering evergreen specimen plant. Also works well in shrub borders and mass plantings. Often successfully used in foundation plantings.
HARDINESS: Zone 5.   **NATIVE HABITAT:** Japan.
SPECIAL CHARACTERISTICS: Many excellent cultivars are available that offer compact growth, variegated foliage, and colorful new growth as well as pink to red flowering varieties. Flower buds for the following spring are formed during the summer and are present through fall and winter, adding seasonal color and interest.

Pinus mugo

SWISS MOUNTAIN PINE

DEER ATTRACTION: Seldomly.
HABIT: Usually low and spreading, but can develop pyramidal and upright forms, especially when grown from seed. Most are very slow growing.
SIZE: Varies. On average most will grow no taller than 15–20' and will spread to up to 30'.
LEAVES: Evergreen, needles 1–3" long, dark green.
FLOWERS: Inconspicuous.
TEXTURE: Medium.
CULTURE: Full sun or partial shade. Prefers moist, rich soil. Partially prune back new growth every year to maintain low compact look. Very susceptible to pine sawflies and scale.
LANDSCAPE/GARDEN VALUE: Usually dwarf varieties are successfully used in foundation plantings, shrub borders, low mass plantings or groupings, and rock gardens.
HARDINESS: Zone 2.   **NATIVE HABITAT:** Mountain regions of Europe.
SPECIAL CHARACTERISTICS: Careful selection must be made when choosing specimens to guarantee desired and uniform height and form since plants grown from seed can produce genetic variations. Only specimens propagated by asexual methods (cuttings, tissue culture, etc.) from known parentage will provide dependable and desired uniformity.

Pyracantha coccinea

FIRETHORN

DEER ATTRACTION: Occasionally.
HABIT: Opens upward and spreads irregularly with thorny growth.
SIZE: 12–15" tall and wide.
LEAVES: Semi-evergreen or evergreen, 1–1 3/4" long, oblong, oval, shiny, dark green.
Flowers: Small 1/3" wide, white. Appears in early June in clusters, 2–3" across.
TEXTURE: Coarse.
CULTURE: Full sun to partial shade. Prefers well drained, slightly acidic soil. Tolerates drought and hot, dry conditions well.
LANDSCAPE/GARDEN VALUE: Often used as a barrier or hedge because of the 1/2–3/4" thorns. Trains well for use on trellises and espaliered on walls.
HARDINESS: Zone 6, can vary with cultivar.
NATIVE HABITAT: Southern Europe and Western Asia.
SPECIAL CHARACTERISTICS: Attractive red, yellow, or orange fruits, depending on cultivar, ripen in September and are loved by birds and other wildlife. Although its rather large thorns may at first give the impression it is very resistant to deer damage, its soft and succulent new growth is often irresistible to deer, making this plant not as good a choice as first thought in many locations, but worth a try.

Skimmia japonica
JAPANESE SKIMMIA

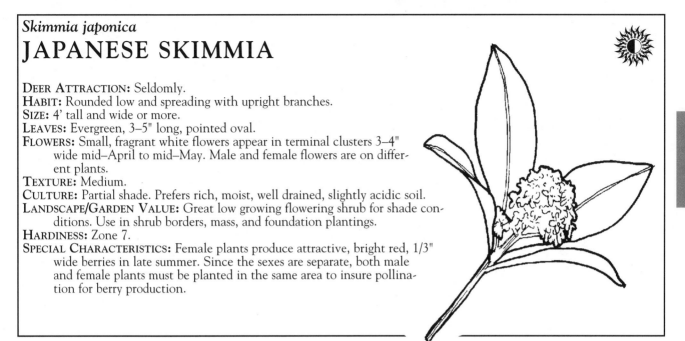

DEER ATTRACTION: Seldomly.
HABIT: Rounded low and spreading with upright branches.
SIZE: 4' tall and wide or more.
LEAVES: Evergreen, 3–5" long, pointed oval.
FLOWERS: Small, fragrant white flowers appear in terminal clusters 3–4"
wide mid–April to mid–May. Male and female flowers are on differ-
ent plants.
TEXTURE: Medium.
CULTURE: Partial shade. Prefers rich, moist, well drained, slightly acidic soil.
LANDSCAPE/GARDEN VALUE: Great low growing flowering shrub for shade con-
ditions. Use in shrub borders, mass, and foundation plantings.
HARDINESS: Zone 7.
SPECIAL CHARACTERISTICS: Female plants produce attractive, bright red, 1/3"
wide berries in late summer. Since the sexes are separate, both male
and female plants must be planted in the same area to insure pollina-
tion for berry production.

Symphoricarpos albus
SNOWBERRY

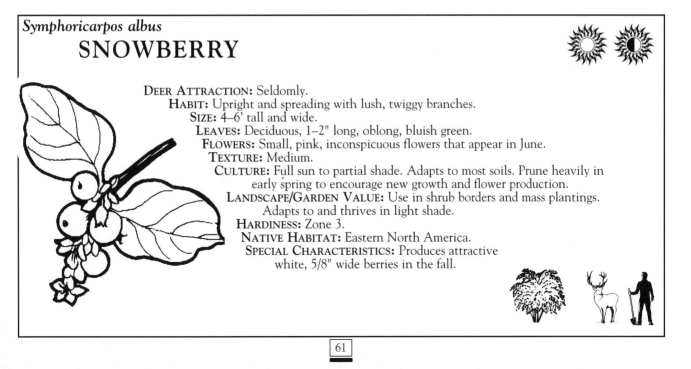

DEER ATTRACTION: Seldomly.
HABIT: Upright and spreading with lush, twiggy branches.
SIZE: 4–6' tall and wide.
LEAVES: Deciduous, 1–2" long, oblong, bluish green.
FLOWERS: Small, pink, inconspicuous flowers that appear in June.
TEXTURE: Medium.
CULTURE: Full sun to partial shade. Adapts to most soils. Prune heavily in
early spring to encourage new growth and flower production.
LANDSCAPE/GARDEN VALUE: Use in shrub borders and mass plantings.
Adapts to and thrives in light shade.
HARDINESS: Zone 3.
NATIVE HABITAT: Eastern North America.
SPECIAL CHARACTERISTICS: Produces attractive
white, 5/8" wide berries in the fall.

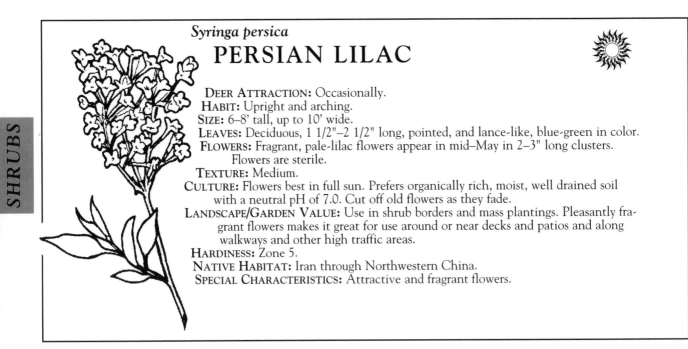

Syringa persica

PERSIAN LILAC

DEER ATTRACTION: Occasionally.
HABIT: Upright and arching.
SIZE: 6–8' tall, up to 10' wide.
LEAVES: Deciduous, 1 1/2"–2 1/2" long, pointed, and lance-like, blue-green in color.
FLOWERS: Fragrant, pale-lilac flowers appear in mid–May in 2–3" long clusters. Flowers are sterile.
TEXTURE: Medium.
CULTURE: Flowers best in full sun. Prefers organically rich, moist, well drained soil with a neutral pH of 7.0. Cut off old flowers as they fade.
LANDSCAPE/GARDEN VALUE: Use in shrub borders and mass plantings. Pleasantly fragrant flowers makes it great for use around or near decks and patios and along walkways and other high traffic areas.
HARDINESS: Zone 5.
NATIVE HABITAT: Iran through Northwestern China.
SPECIAL CHARACTERISTICS: Attractive and fragrant flowers.

Viburnum carlessii

KOREANSPICE VIBURNUM

DEER ATTRACTION: Occasionally.
HABIT: Rounded with upright and spreading branches.
SIZE: 6–8' tall and wide.
LEAVES: Deciduous, 1–4" broad oval, dull green color with serrated edge.
FLOWERS: Fragrant, pink, 2/5–3/5" wide, appear in 2–3" wide clusters in late April to early May.
TEXTURE: Medium.
CULTURE: Full sun to partial shade. Prefers rich, moist, well drained soil that is slightly acidic (below 6.5).
LANDSCAPE/GARDEN VALUE: Great for use in shrub borders and mass plantings. Pleasantly fragrant flowers make it great for use around or near decks and patios and along walkways and other high traffic areas.
HARDINESS: Zone 4.
NATIVE HABITAT: Korea.
SPECIAL CHARACTERISTICS: One of the best of the fragrant viburnums.

Ajuga reptans
BUGLEWEED

DEER ATTRACTION: Rarely.
HABIT: Low, fast spreading ground cover.
SIZE: 4–12" tall.
LEAVES: Evergreen, 4" long, round to oval. Foliage is available in several colors that include green, bronze, deep purple, and variegated.
FLOWERS: Compact, 2–4" upright spikes that appear in May through June and are available in blue, white, and purplish red.
TEXTURE: Medium.
CULTURE: Full sun to shade. Adapts to most well drained soils.
LANDSCAPE/ GARDEN VALUE: Primarily used as a ground cover.
HARDINESS: Zone 2.
SPECIAL CHARACTERISTICS: A member of the mint family. Fancy varieties may freely self seed the area they are planted in; however, seedlings may not look like parents but will usually revert back to species. Therefore, unwanted seedlings may need to be selectively removed or the area may need to be replanted every few years.

Arctostaphyllos uva-ursi
BEARBERRY

DEER ATTRACTION: Rarely.
HABIT: Low growing, evergreen ground cover.
SIZE: 6–12" tall and 2–4' wide.
LEAVES: Evergreen, 1/2" wide, oblong to round. Very shiny, dark green on top, lighter beneath. Turns red to bronze in the fall and winter.
FLOWERS: Tiny whitish pink, 1/6" long bell-shaped flowers appear in April and early May.
TEXTURE: Fine.
CULTURE: Full sun or partial shade. Adapts well to almost any well drained soil. Prefers acidic soils (pH of 4.5–5.5) and tolerates salt and seaside conditions. Does not like fertilization and excessive watering. Seems to thrive on neglect.
LANDSCAPE/ GARDEN VALUE: Primarily used as a ground cover.
HARDINESS: Zone 2.
NATIVE HABITAT: Europe, Asia, and North America.
SPECIAL CHARACTERISTICS: Good fall color. One of the best ground covers for use where deer browsing is a severe problem.

GROUND COVERS

Convallaria majalis
LILY-OF-THE-VALLEY

DEER ATTRACTION: Rarely.
HABIT: Low, spreading ground cover.
SIZE: 8" high.
LEAVES: 8" long, 1–3" wide, oval. Leaves die to ground completely in fall.
FLOWERS: Upright spikes with white, 1/4" wide, waxy, hanging, bell-like flowers that are pleasantly fragrant and appear in mid–May through mid–June.
TEXTURE: Medium.
CULTURE: Thrives in shade. Prefers rich, moist, well drained soil. Responds well to yearly application of an organic fertilizer in spring, but once established, beds require little or no other maintenance.
LANDSCAPE/ GARDEN VALUE: Good ground cover for shade.
HARDINESS: Zone 2.
NATIVE HABITAT: Europe, Asia, and Eastern North America.
SPECIAL CHARACTERISTICS: Low maintenance ground cover. A pink flowering variety, "Rosea" is also available. Propagated and grown from rhizomes (modified underground stem).

Epimedium grandiflorum
BARRENWORT

DEER ATTRACTION: Rarely.
HABIT: Dense, low, and spreading ground cover.
SIZE: 9–12" tall, spreading to 12" or more.
LEAVES: 2–3" long, 1–2" wide pointed, heart-shaped leaflets. Leaves are compound with 3 leaflets to a leaf. In spring, leaves are red, dark green through summer turning bronze in fall.
FLOWERS: 1–1 1/2" wide, spidery, purplish-pink flowers with white spurs appear on 12" long, loose clusters from May through June.
TEXTURE: Medium.
CULTURE: Prefers partial shade, rich, moist, well drained soil.
LANDSCAPE/ GARDEN VALUE: Great flowering ground cover for partial shade.
HARDINESS: Zone 3.
NATIVE HABITAT: Japan, Korea, and Northeastern Asia.
SPECIAL CHARACTERISTICS: Several other varieties are available with white or pink flowers. Offers good autumn color (bronze).

Lamium maculatum

DEAD NETTLE

DEER ATTRACTION: Rarely.
HABIT: Dense, low, and spreading ground cover.
SIZE: 6–12" tall, spreading to 18" or more.
LEAVES: 1 1/2–2 1/2" long, oval, heart-shaped, crinkled with serrated edge. Leaves are green with silvery white splotches.
FLOWERS: 1–2" long, purplish-pink flowers appear throughout the summer.
TEXTURE: Medium.
CULTURE: Prefers partial shade and rich, moist, well drained soil.
LANDSCAPE/ GARDEN VALUE: Great flowering ground cover for partial shade.
HARDINESS: Zone 2.
NATIVE HABITAT: Europe.
SPECIAL CHARACTERISTICS: Blooms throughout most of the summer. White flowering varieties are available. May become invasive. Silvery, light colored foliage lightens up dark, shady areas and contrasts well with dark green evergreens. An attractive background for taller and colorful plants.

GROUND COVERS

Pachysandra terminalis

PACHYSANDRA OR JAPANESE SPURGE

DEER ATTRACTION: Rarely.
HABIT: Low spreading ground cover.
SIZE: 6–12" tall, spreading to 18" or more.
LEAVES: 2–3" dark green, shiny, and deeply serrated oval. Foliage remains through winter.
FLOWERS: 2–3" white, upright spikes appear in early May, but not very showy.
TEXTURE: Medium.
CULTURE: Shade to part sun. Prefers rich, moist, well drained, slightly acidic soil but will adapt well to a wide variety of locations except constant hot, dry, sunny areas, but will tolerate dry shade. Plants are stoloniferous and can spread rapidly when fertilized regularly.
LANDSCAPE/ GARDEN VALUE: Great ground cover for shady areas, especially under and around trees and shrubs where competition from roots may cause soil to stay dry near the surface.
HARDINESS: Zone 5. **NATIVE HABITAT:** Japan.
SPECIAL CHARACTERISTICS: Produces white, inconspicuous fruits-berries in fall. Probably the most commonly found ground cover. Despite its ubiquitous nature, pachysandra is one of the most dependable ground covers for use in the deer resistant garden or landscape.

Santolina chamaecyparissus

LAVENDER-COTTON

DEER ATTRACTION: Rarely.
HABIT: Low, shrubby.
SIZE: 1 1/2–2' tall and wide.
LEAVES: 1/2–3/4" long, lance-like, aromatic and silvery gray.
FLOWERS: Small yellow flowers appear in 1/2–3/4" clusters in July and August.
TEXTURE: Fine.
CULTURE: Full sun. Prefers poor sandy or gravely soils. Tolerates hot and very dry conditions.
LANDSCAPE/ GARDEN VALUE: Use as a ground cover or border edge. Great for rock and wall gardens.
HARDINESS: Zones 6–7.
NATIVE HABITAT: Southern Europe.
SPECIAL CHARACTERISTICS: Its aromatic foliage acts as a deer repellent. Herbal uses include its household use as a moth repellent and its oil being used to make perfume.

Sempervirens tectorum

HENS-AND-CHICKS

DEER ATTRACTION: Rarely.
HABIT: Very low, ground hugging ground cover.
SIZE: 8–12" tall and wide.
LEAVES: 1/4–1/2" bluntly pointed ovals that tightly circle its center forming a densely crowded rosette of grayish green leaves, often red tipped, 3–4" across.
FLOWERS: 3/4–1" across, clusters of pink-purple flowers appear on 8–12" hairy stalks infrequently throughout the summer.
TEXTURE: Coarse.
CULTURE: Full sun. Likes hot, dry, poor soils. Plants multiply rapidly by forming smaller plants at their base, therefore forming continuously spreading mats of dense rosettes.
LANDSCAPE/ GARDEN VALUE: Excellent ground cover for hot, dry, sunny areas. Suitable for rock gardens. Use in crevices of rock walls and between stones in paths.
HARDINESS: Zone 4.
NATIVE HABITAT: Europe and Asia.
SPECIAL CHARACTERISTICS: Cultivated since the 16th century, Hens-and-Chicks are very hardy and durable and can be effective in areas where the extremes of sun, heat, and dryness won't allow anything else to cover the ground adequately.

Vinca minor
PERIWINKLE OR MYRTLE

DEER ATTRACTION: Rarely.
HABIT: Low, spreading ground cover.
SIZE: 4–6" tall.
LEAVES: 2" long, dark green, shiny ovals.
FLOWERS: 3/4" across, lavender-blue flowers in late April.
TEXTURE: Medium.
CULTURE: Full sun to deep shade. Will tolerate almost any but the poorest soils. Reproduces easily since stems root readily where it comes in contact with soil.
LANDSCAPE/ GARDEN VALUE: Good ground cover for almost any area.
Hardiness: Zone 4.
NATIVE HABITAT: Europe and Western Asia.
SPECIAL CHARACTERISTICS: Like pachysandra, it's rather ubiquitous in gardens and landscapes, however, its resistance to deer browsing is often unsurpassed and therefore is of value in the deer resistant garden or landscape.

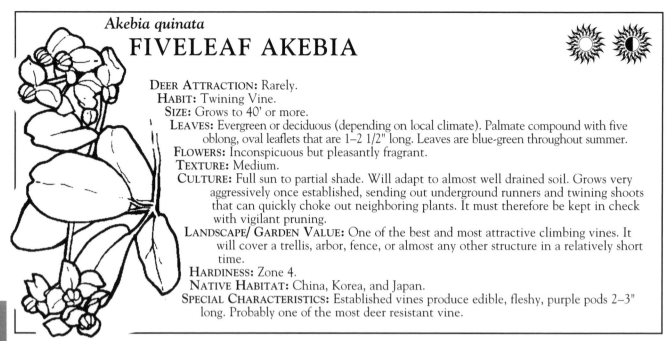

Akebia quinata

FIVELEAF AKEBIA

DEER ATTRACTION: Rarely.
HABIT: Twining Vine.
SIZE: Grows to 40' or more.
LEAVES: Evergreen or deciduous (depending on local climate). Palmate compound with five oblong, oval leaflets that are 1–2 1/2" long. Leaves are blue-green throughout summer.
FLOWERS: Inconspicuous but pleasantly fragrant.
TEXTURE: Medium.
CULTURE: Full sun to partial shade. Will adapt to almost well drained soil. Grows very aggressively once established, sending out underground runners and twining shoots that can quickly choke out neighboring plants. It must therefore be kept in check with vigilant pruning.
LANDSCAPE/ GARDEN VALUE: One of the best and most attractive climbing vines. It will cover a trellis, arbor, fence, or almost any other structure in a relatively short time.
HARDINESS: Zone 4.
NATIVE HABITAT: China, Korea, and Japan.
SPECIAL CHARACTERISTICS: Established vines produce edible, fleshy, purple pods 2–3" long. Probably one of the most deer resistant vine.

Campsis radicans

TRUMPET VINE

DEER ATTRACTION: Occasionally.
HABIT: Clinging, shrubby vine.
SIZE: Grows to over 50' or more.
LEAVES: Deciduous, brilliant green compound leaf, 6–8" long with 9–11 leaflets that are 1 1/4–1 1/2" long with serrated edges.
FLOWERS: 2–4" long, orange, trumpet shaped flowers grouped in clusters of 4–12 that begin to appear in July and continue through September.
TEXTURE: Medium.
CULTURE: Full sun and almost any type of soil. A very tough, vigorous grower with little or minimum care. Often spreads by underground runners.
LANDSCAPE/ GARDEN VALUE: A vigorous flowering vine for covering a trellis, arbor, fence, wall, or other structure.
HARDINESS: Zone 4.
NATIVE HABITAT: Mid-Atlantic of United States, south to Florida and west to Texas.
SPECIAL CHARACTERISTICS: Holds to objects using aerial rootlets (holdfasts) that cling to structures. Handling leaves or flowers may cause dermatitis.

VINES

Celastrus scandens
BITTERSWEET

DEER ATTRACTION: Seldomly.
HABIT: Twining vine.
SIZE: Grows to 20' or more.
LEAVES: Deciduous, 2–4" long, pointed, oval. Shiny, bright green in summer, yellow fall color.
FLOWERS: Inconspicuous.
TEXTURE: Medium in leaf, coarse when leafless.
CULTURE: Full sun to partial shade. Adapts to almost any soil. Grows very vigorously when planted in good soil.
LANDSCAPE/ GARDEN VALUE: A very fast growing, twining vine that is usually used or allowed to ramble over fences, walls, rock piles, dead or live tree trunks, or any other structure, or eyesore.
HARDINESS: Zone 3.
NATIVE HABITAT: Canada, south to Mexico and east of the Rockies.
SPECIAL CHARACTERISTICS: Yellow fruit with crimson seeds appear in October that provide ornamental value and is often harvested and used in dried flower arrangements.

Polygonum aubertii
SILVER LACE VINE

DEER ATTRACTION: Occasionally.
HABIT: Twining vine.
SIZE: Grows to 35' or more.
LEAVES: Deciduous, 1 1/2–2 1/2" long, oblong, oval with undulating leaf margin. Leaves are bright green through summer, new growth is reddish bronze turning to green.
FLOWERS: Small, 1/4" wide, fragrant white flowers appear in short panicles in July through September.
TEXTURE: Medium in leaf, otherwise coarse.
CULTURE: Full sun or shade. Adapts to almost any soil. Tolerates very dry soils. Once established it is a vigorous grower.
LANDSCAPE/ GARDEN VALUE: A good, quick growing vine that adapts well to poor conditions where other vines fail to thrive. It will quickly cover a fence, arbor, or any other structure.
HARDINESS: Zone 4.
NATIVE HABITAT: China.
SPECIAL CHARACTERISTICS: Susceptible to Japanese Beetle damage.

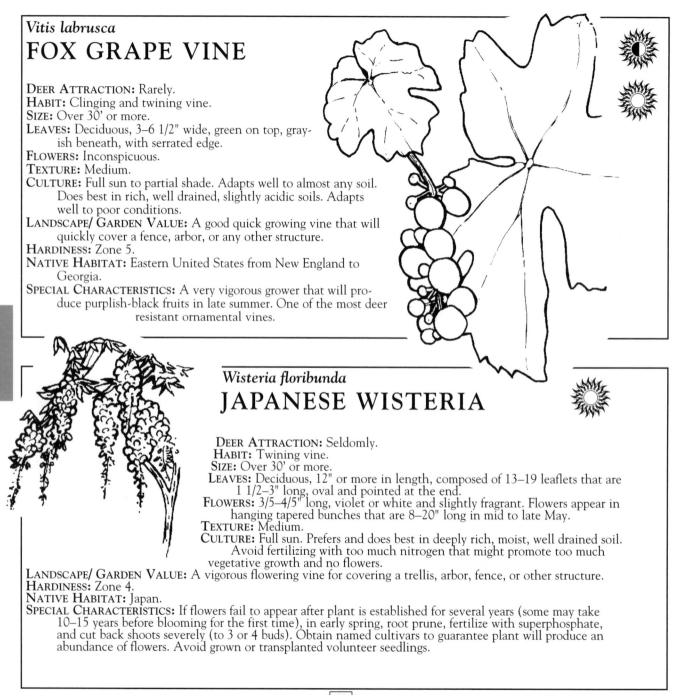

Vitis labrusca

FOX GRAPE VINE

DEER ATTRACTION: Rarely.
HABIT: Clinging and twining vine.
SIZE: Over 30' or more.
LEAVES: Deciduous, 3–6 1/2" wide, green on top, gray-ish beneath, with serrated edge.
FLOWERS: Inconspicuous.
TEXTURE: Medium.
CULTURE: Full sun to partial shade. Adapts well to almost any soil. Does best in rich, well drained, slightly acidic soils. Adapts well to poor conditions.
LANDSCAPE/ GARDEN VALUE: A good quick growing vine that will quickly cover a fence, arbor, or any other structure.
HARDINESS: Zone 5.
NATIVE HABITAT: Eastern United States from New England to Georgia.
SPECIAL CHARACTERISTICS: A very vigorous grower that will produce purplish-black fruits in late summer. One of the most deer resistant ornamental vines.

Wisteria floribunda

JAPANESE WISTERIA

DEER ATTRACTION: Seldomly.
HABIT: Twining vine.
SIZE: Over 30' or more.
LEAVES: Deciduous, 12" or more in length, composed of 13–19 leaflets that are 1 1/2–3" long, oval and pointed at the end.
FLOWERS: 3/5–4/5" long, violet or white and slightly fragrant. Flowers appear in hanging tapered bunches that are 8–20" long in mid to late May.
TEXTURE: Medium.
CULTURE: Full sun. Prefers and does best in deeply rich, moist, well drained soil. Avoid fertilizing with too much nitrogen that might promote too much vegetative growth and no flowers.
LANDSCAPE/ GARDEN VALUE: A vigorous flowering vine for covering a trellis, arbor, fence, or other structure.
HARDINESS: Zone 4.
NATIVE HABITAT: Japan.
SPECIAL CHARACTERISTICS: If flowers fail to appear after plant is established for several years (some may take 10–15 years before blooming for the first time), in early spring, root prune, fertilize with superphosphate, and cut back shoots severely (to 3 or 4 buds). Obtain named cultivars to guarantee plant will produce an abundance of flowers. Avoid grown or transplanted volunteer seedlings.

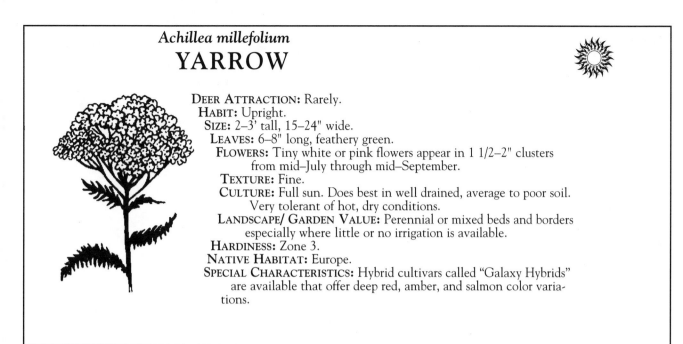

Achillea millefolium
YARROW

DEER ATTRACTION: Rarely.
HABIT: Upright.
SIZE: 2–3' tall, 15–24" wide.
LEAVES: 6–8" long, feathery green.
FLOWERS: Tiny white or pink flowers appear in 1 1/2–2" clusters from mid–July through mid–September.
TEXTURE: Fine.
CULTURE: Full sun. Does best in well drained, average to poor soil. Very tolerant of hot, dry conditions.
LANDSCAPE/ GARDEN VALUE: Perennial or mixed beds and borders especially where little or no irrigation is available.
HARDINESS: Zone 3.
NATIVE HABITAT: Europe.
SPECIAL CHARACTERISTICS: Hybrid cultivars called "Galaxy Hybrids" are available that offer deep red, amber, and salmon color variations.

Aconitum carmichaelii
MONKSHOOD

DEER ATTRACTION: Rarely.
HABIT: Upright.
SIZE: 4–6' tall, 18–24" wide.
LEAVES: 2–3" wide, 3 lobed, leathery dark green leaves, similar to *Delphinium elatum* (p76).
FLOWERS: Blue, violet, lavender, depending on cultivar, appear on 6" compact spikes in August and September.
TEXTURE: Medium.
CULTURE: Full sun, but will do quite well in partial shade. Prefers moist, well drained soil. Will not tolerate hot, dry conditions too well. Often needs to be staked.
LANDSCAPE/ GARDEN VALUE: A tall growing perennial, use in perennial or mixed borders as a background plant. Best used in masses. Contrasts well with yellow and white flowering plants.
HARDINESS: Zone 3.
NATIVE HABITAT: Eastern Asia.
SPECIAL CHARACTERISTICS: All parts are poisonous making it extremely deer resistant.

Arabis caucasica
ROCK-CRESS

DEER ATTRACTION: Rarely.
HABIT: Low and spreading often forming mats.
SIZE: 6–10" tall, spreads 18" or more.
LEAVES: 1–3" wide, with a fine white-gray fuzz.
FLOWERS: Fragrant white, no more than 1/2" wide, appear in early spring.
TEXTURE: Fine.
CULTURE: Full sun. Prefers moist, well drained soils, but will tolerate dry conditions.
LANDSCAPE/ GARDEN VALUE: Good for edging borders or beds. Use in rock and wall gardens.
HARDINESS: Zone 3.
NATIVE HABITAT: Europe (Caucasus area).
SPECIAL CHARACTERISTICS: Variegated leaved and double pink and white flowering varieties are available.

Artemisia schmidtiana
WORMWOOD

DEER ATTRACTION: Rarely.
HABIT: Low and spreading, often forming mounds.
SIZE: 1–2' tall, 18" or more wide.
LEAVES: Silvery gray, deeply cut leaves are covered with a very fine fuzz.
FLOWERS: Inconspicuous.
TEXTURE: Very fine.
CULTURE: Full sun and moist, liking well drained to poor, dry soils. Cut back hard in late summer to rejuvenate foliage growth.
LANDSCAPE/ GARDEN VALUE: Use as edging or ground cover.
HARDINESS: Zone 2.
SPECIAL CHARACTERISTICS: Over the years it forms mounds that tend to thin out in the middle and therefore needs to be dug up, divided, and replanted every few years.

Asclepias tuberosa
BUTTERFLY MILKWEED

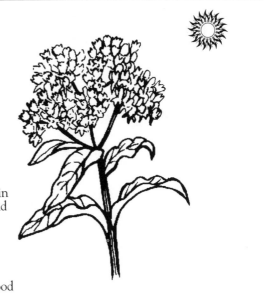

DEER ATTRACTION: Rarely.
HABIT: Upright.
SIZE: 3' tall, 18" wide.
LEAVES: 2–6" long and lance-like, green covered with short, stiff hairs.
FLOWERS: 1/3" wide, orange, appear in showy clusters above plant in August and September.
TEXTURE: Medium.
CULTURE: Full sun. Does well in dry, sandy soils.
LANDSCAPE/ GARDEN VALUE: A popular flowering perennial. Use in sunny perennial and mixed borders. Great for use on banks and berms where soils may tend to dry quickly. A native wildflower.
HARDINESS: Zone 3.
NATIVE HABITAT: Meadows of Eastern United States from Maine to Florida.
SPECIAL CHARACTERISTICS: Flowers attract butterflies and make good long lasting cut flowers.

Aster novi-belgi
NEW YORK ASTERS

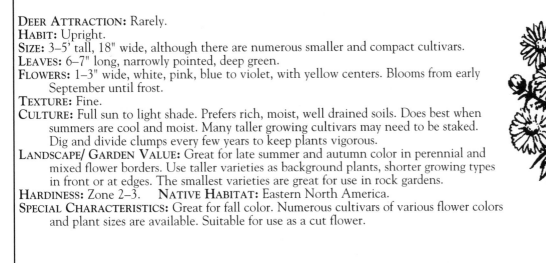

DEER ATTRACTION: Rarely.
HABIT: Upright.
SIZE: 3–5' tall, 18" wide, although there are numerous smaller and compact cultivars.
LEAVES: 6–7" long, narrowly pointed, deep green.
FLOWERS: 1–3" wide, white, pink, blue to violet, with yellow centers. Blooms from early September until frost.
TEXTURE: Fine.
CULTURE: Full sun to light shade. Prefers rich, moist, well drained soils. Does best when summers are cool and moist. Many taller growing cultivars may need to be staked. Dig and divide clumps every few years to keep plants vigorous.
LANDSCAPE/ GARDEN VALUE: Great for late summer and autumn color in perennial and mixed flower borders. Use taller varieties as background plants, shorter growing types in front or at edges. The smallest varieties are great for use in rock gardens.
HARDINESS: Zone 2–3.   **NATIVE HABITAT:** Eastern North America.
SPECIAL CHARACTERISTICS: Great for fall color. Numerous cultivars of various flower colors and plant sizes are available. Suitable for use as a cut flower.

Astilbe x arendsii
HYBRID ASTILBE

DEER ATTRACTION: Rarely.
HABIT: Upright.
SIZE: 2–4' tall, 2 -3' wide. Sizes vary according to cultivar.
LEAVES: 6–18" long, compound, green although some cultivars have bronze leaves.
FLOWERS: Very small, appearing on 6–12" upright feathery spikes, in shades of white, light pink to deep red and lavender. Blooming occurs from late May to August, depending on cultivar.
TEXTURE: Fine.
CULTURE: Prefers partial shade. Likes cool, moist, rich, well drained soil. Can be grown in full sun but need adequate moisture levels maintained to avoid leaf scorching and reduced vigor.
LANDSCAPE/ GARDEN VALUE: A popular flowering perennial for shade. Use in shady perennial and mixed beds and borders.
HARDINESS: Zones 5–8.
NATIVE HABITAT: These hybrids come from Germany.
SPECIAL CHARACTERISTICS: Over 30 cultivars are available.

Aubretia deltoidea
PURPLE ROCK-CRESS

DEER ATTRACTION: Rarely.
HABIT: Low and spreading, often forming mats.
SIZE: 6–8" high, spreading to 18" or more.
LEAVES: 1" long gray-green, oval to spoon shaped with serrated edges, covered with tiny hairs.
FLOWERS: 3/4" wide with four petals. Comes in shades of mostly blue, but purples and reds are also common. Blooms April through June.
TEXTURE: Fine.
CULTURE: Full sun. Prefers poor, well drained, rocky soils. Does best in cooler climates. Cut back hard after first bloom when flowers fade to keep growth compact and encourage secondary bloom.
LANDSCAPE/ GARDEN VALUE: Use as edging in sunny beds and borders. Great for use in rock gardens and in crevices of rock walls.
HARDINESS: Zone 5–7.
NATIVE HABITAT: Europe and Asia Minor.

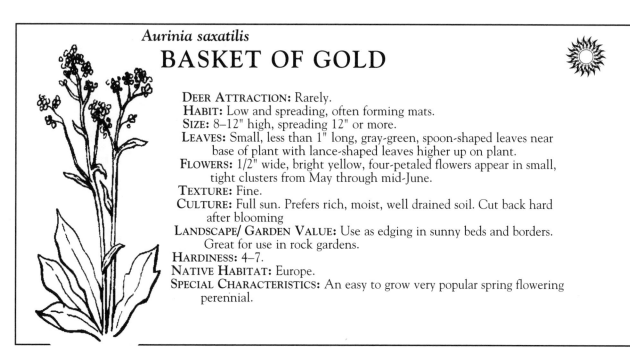

Aurinia saxatilis

BASKET OF GOLD

DEER ATTRACTION: Rarely.
HABIT: Low and spreading, often forming mats.
SIZE: 8–12" high, spreading 12" or more.
LEAVES: Small, less than 1" long, gray-green, spoon-shaped leaves near base of plant with lance-shaped leaves higher up on plant.
FLOWERS: 1/2" wide, bright yellow, four-petaled flowers appear in small, tight clusters from May through mid-June.
TEXTURE: Fine.
CULTURE: Full sun. Prefers rich, moist, well drained soil. Cut back hard after blooming
LANDSCAPE/ GARDEN VALUE: Use as edging in sunny beds and borders. Great for use in rock gardens.
HARDINESS: 4–7.
NATIVE HABITAT: Europe.
SPECIAL CHARACTERISTICS: An easy to grow very popular spring flowering perennial.

Coreopsis lanceolata

LANCE COREOPSIS

DEER ATTRACTION: Rarely.
HABIT: Upright.
SIZE: 2' tall, 18" wide.
LEAVES: 1 1/2–2" long, lance-like, green, and borne on lower half of the plant.
FLOWERS: 2 1/2" across, yellow, appear throughout the summer.
TEXTURE: Fine.
CULTURE: Full sun. Does well in almost any garden soil. Prefers dry, light soils. Constantly remove faded flowers to encourage new ones.
LANDSCAPE/ GARDEN VALUE: Use in sunny perennial and mixed beds and borders. Great for rock gardens and wildflower gardens.
HARDINESS: Zone 3–9.
NATIVE HABITAT: Eastern North America.
SPECIAL CHARACTERISTICS: A native wildflower.

Delphinium elatum

LARKSPUR

DEER ATTRACTION: Rarely.
HABIT: Upright.
SIZE: 4–6' tall, 2" wide.
LEAVES: 3–5" palmate, serrated edges, green.
FLOWERS: 1–2" wide, blue or purple, single or double flowers. Blooms appear in June and July. Hybrids offer more color variations of blue, violet, purple, pink, and white.
TEXTURE: Coarse.
CULTURE: Full sun. Grows best in rich, moist, well drained and slightly alkaline soils. Prefers cool, moist summers. Plant in areas protected from wind or provide sturdy stakes. Flower stalks are especially brittle and need staking. Responds well to heavy feeding. Constantly remove faded flowers to encourage new ones.
LANDSCAPE/ GARDEN VALUE: Use as a background plant in perennial beds and borders.
HARDINESS: Zone 2–9.
NATIVE HABITAT: Siberia.
SPECIAL CHARACTERISTICS: Considered a short-lived perennial, many treat *Delphiniums* as an annual or biennial. Suitable for use as a cut flower.

Echinacea purpurea

PURPLE CONEFLOWER

DEER ATTRACTION: Rarely.
HABIT: Upright.
SIZE: 2–4' tall, spreads to 18" or more.
LEAVES: 2–3" long, lance-shaped, green with serrated edges.
FLOWERS: 2 1/2–3" wide, purple or white daisy-like flowers that appear in July and August.
TEXTURE: Coarse.
CULTURE: Full sun. Does well in almost any well drained fertile soil.
LANDSCAPE/ GARDEN VALUE: Use in sunny perennial or mixed beds and borders or wildflower gardens.
HARDINESS: Zones 3–9.
NATIVE HABITAT: North America.
SPECIAL CHARACTERISTICS: A native North American wildflower. Suitable for use as a cut flower.

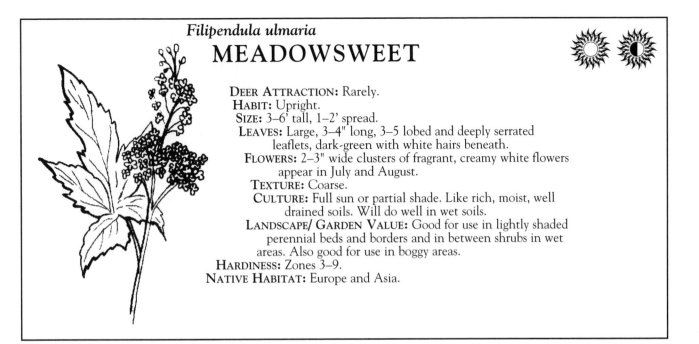

Filipendula ulmaria
MEADOWSWEET

DEER ATTRACTION: Rarely.
HABIT: Upright.
SIZE: 3–6' tall, 1–2' spread.
LEAVES: Large, 3–4" long, 3–5 lobed and deeply serrated leaflets, dark-green with white hairs beneath.
FLOWERS: 2–3" wide clusters of fragrant, creamy white flowers appear in July and August.
TEXTURE: Coarse.
CULTURE: Full sun or partial shade. Like rich, moist, well drained soils. Will do well in wet soils.
LANDSCAPE/ GARDEN VALUE: Good for use in lightly shaded perennial beds and borders and in between shrubs in wet areas. Also good for use in boggy areas.
HARDINESS: Zones 3–9.
NATIVE HABITAT: Europe and Asia.

Geranium
CRANESBILL

DEER ATTRACTION: Rarely.
HABIT: This group of plants is comprised of members (over 400 species) that exhibit various habits from low and spreading to upright.
SIZE: 6–36" tall, 8–36" spread.
LEAVES: Small, many lobes, and green.
FLOWERS: 1/2–2" across with 5 petals. Colors range from white, pink, blue, to purple. Bloom time varies among species, late spring, summer and fall.
TEXTURE: Fine.
CULTURE: Full sun. Adapts to almost any well drained soil. Cut back hard after first flowers fade to encourage more. Taller species may need staking. Dig and divide every 3–4 years to rejuvenate. Most are very insect and disease free.
LANDSCAPE/ GARDEN VALUE: Use as goundcovers, in perennial beds and borders and as accent plants around shrubs. A large group that contains many species are useful in various situations.
HARDINESS: Zone 4–8 depending on specie.
NATIVE HABITAT: North America, Asia, and Europe.

PERENNIALS

Helenium autumnale
SNEEZEWEED

DEER ATTRACTION: Rarely.
HABIT: Upright, forming a clump.
SIZE: 3–6' tall, 2–3' wide.
LEAVES: 5–6" long, lance-like with serrated edge, and green. Leaves extend down and along stem giving stem a winged look.
FLOWERS: 2" wide, yellow, drooping, almost daisy-like flower with terminal end of petals notched. Blooms in August through October.
TEXTURE: Medium.
CULTURE: Full sun. Adapts to almost any well drained soil. Often needs staking. Dig and divide every 3 years to rejuvenate clumps.
LANDSCAPE/ GARDEN VALUE: Use in perennial beds and borders and wildflower gardens.
HARDINESS: Zone 3–8.
NATIVE HABITAT: Eastern North America.
SPECIAL CHARACTERISTICS: Suitable for use as a cut flower.

PERENNIALS

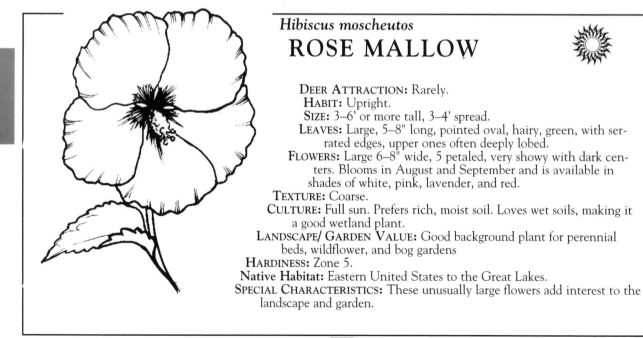

Hibiscus moscheutos
ROSE MALLOW

DEER ATTRACTION: Rarely.
HABIT: Upright.
SIZE: 3–6' or more tall, 3–4' spread.
LEAVES: Large, 5–8" long, pointed oval, hairy, green, with serrated edges, upper ones often deeply lobed.
FLOWERS: Large 6–8" wide, 5 petaled, very showy with dark centers. Blooms in August and September and is available in shades of white, pink, lavender, and red.
TEXTURE: Coarse.
CULTURE: Full sun. Prefers rich, moist soil. Loves wet soils, making it a good wetland plant.
LANDSCAPE/ GARDEN VALUE: Good background plant for perennial beds, wildflower, and bog gardens
HARDINESS: Zone 5.
Native Habitat: Eastern United States to the Great Lakes.
SPECIAL CHARACTERISTICS: These unusually large flowers add interest to the landscape and garden.

Lychnis coronaria
ROSE CAMPION

DEER ATTRACTION: Rarely.
HABIT: Upright.
SIZE: 2–3' tall, 18" wide.
LEAVES: 4" long, oval covered with gray woolly fuzz giving the
    plant a silvery appearance.
FLOWERS: 1" wide, bright crimson, red–pink flowers appear in
    clusters in June and July.
TEXTURE: Medium.
CULTURE: Full sun to partial shade. Likes almost any well
    drained soil.
LANDSCAPE/ GARDEN VALUE: Use in perennial beds and borders.
HARDINESS: Zones 4–8.
NATIVE HABITAT: Southern Europe.
SPECIAL CHARACTERISTICS: Silvery foliage provides good contrast
    and lightens shaded areas.

Lysimachia clethroides
JAPANESE LOOSESTRIFE

DEER ATTRACTION: Rarely.
HABIT: Upright.
SIZE: 2–3' tall and wide.
LEAVES: 3–6" long lance-shaped, gray-green.
FLOWERS: 1/2" wide, white, appear on dense, 6–8" long, curved spikes.
TEXTURE: Coarse.
CULTURE: Full sun or partial shade. Prefers moist soils. Remove faded flowers to
    prevent it from seeding itself.
LANDSCAPE/ GARDEN VALUE: Mostly used in perennial borders and bog gardens.
HARDINESS: Zone 3–8.
NATIVE HABITAT: Japan and China.
SPECIAL CHARACTERISTICS: Can become invasive if neglected.

Lythrum salicaria
PURPLE LOOSESTRIFE

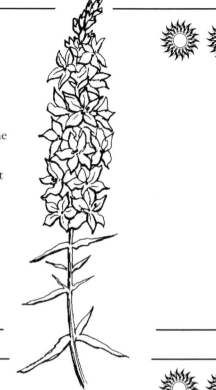

DEER ATTRACTION: Rarely.
HABIT: Upright.
SIZE: 2–5' tall, spreading 2' or more.
LEAVES: 3–6" long, lance-like, green.
FLOWERS: 3/4" wide, reddish–purple flowers appear on 1' tall spikes in June through September.
TEXTURE: Coarse.
CULTURE: Full sun or partial shade. Likes wet soil but will adapt to almost any soil.
LANDSCAPE/ GARDEN VALUE: Use in sunny perennial borders and bog garden. Can become very invasive if not carefully kept in check.
HARDINESS: Zone 3–9.
NATIVE HABITAT: Europe and Asia.
SPECIAL CHARACTERISTICS: A very easy to grow perennial, maybe too easy. It can become a weed problem and several states in the Midwest have banned its sale.

Monarda didyma
BEEBALM

DEER ATTRACTION: Rarely.
HABIT: Upright.
SIZE: 2–3' tall, spreads to 18" or more.
LEAVES: 3–6" long, oval, hairy, with serrated edge and aromatic.
FLOWERS: 2" wide, bright red blooms from June through August.
TEXTURE: Medium.
CULTURE: Full sun or partial shade. Prefers moist, rich, well drained soils. Remove faded flowers frequently to encourage more flowers.
LANDSCAPE/ GARDEN VALUE: Use in sunny perennial beds and borders, bog gardens, and other wet areas.
HARDINESS: Zone 4–9.
NATIVE HABITAT: Eastern United States.
SPECIAL CHARACTERISTICS: Attracts bees, butterflies, and hummingbirds. It is also considered an herb and is used to make teas, oils (Bergamot), and perfumes. The oil is an ingredient of Earl Grey tea.

Paeonia officinalis
COMMON PEONY

DEER ATTRACTION: Rarely.
HABIT: Upright.
SIZE: 3' tall and wide.
LEAVES: 12" or more long, consisting of two groups of three 4–6" leaflets. Bonze buds emerge from ground in spring, turning to green, leathery leaves.
FLOWERS: 4" across, ranging from deep red, pink, to shades of white. Flowers are available in single or double forms and appear in late May.
TEXTURE: Medium.
CULTURE: Full sun. Prefers well prepared soils that are moist, well drained and enriched with compost or well rotted cow manure. Care should be taken when planting to make sure crowns (where buds emerge) are no deeper than 2" or plants may fail to bloom. Peonies respond well to a side-dressing of well rotted cow manure in early spring and after blooming.
LANDSCAPE/ GARDEN VALUE: An old-fashioned favorite. Makes an excellent choice for a sunny mixed border.

Perovskia x hybrida
RUSSIAN SAGE

DEER ATTRACTION: Rarely.
HABIT: Upright, very shrublike.
SIZE: 3–4' tall, spreading to over 3'.
LEAVES: 2–3" long, lance-like, that can be variably cut and toothed and finely divided, green-gray in color.
FLOWERS: Small purplish-blue, appear on 3–6" loose and hairy spikes that appear in mid to late summer.
TEXTURE: Fine.
CULTURE: Full sun. Adapts to almost any well drained soil. Plants should be cut back to several inches from the ground in early spring to encourage dense growth and flowering.
LANDSCAPE/ GARDEN VALUE: Great for contrast in sunny perennial or mixed beds and borders.
HARDINESS: Zones 5–9.
NATIVE HABITAT: Eastern Asia.
SPECIAL CHARACTERISTICS: Loose, hairy flowers, and its fine foliage give this shrublike plant a smokey blue appearance that contrasts well with large, yellow or daisy-like flowers.

PERENNIALS

Polemonium caeruleum
JACOB'S LADDER

DEER ATTRACTION: Rarely.
HABIT: Upright.
SIZE: 15–24" tall, spreads to over 18".
LEAVES: 4–6" long leaves made up of as many as 20–27 pairs of small, evenly spaced 1/2–1" long leaflets.
FLOWERS: 1" wide, cup-like blue flowers appear in late May through July.
TEXTURE: Fine.
CULTURE: Prefers to grow in partial shade and rich soil. Remove faded flowers to encourage more blooms.
LANDSCAPE/ GARDEN VALUE: Use in partially shaded perennial and mixed beds and borders.
HARDINESS: Zones 3–8.
NATIVE HABITAT: Europe.
SPECIAL CHARACTERISTICS: The evenly spaced leaflets of the leaves look like the rungs of a ladder, therefore its common name, Jacob's Ladder.

Rudbeckia maxima
BLACK-EYED SUSAN

DEER ATTRACTION: Rarely.
HABIT: Upright.
SIZE: 5–6' tall, 2' wide.
LEAVES: Up to 12" long, oval to spoon shaped, hairy, grayish-green leaves with serrated edges.
FLOWERS: Up to 5–6" wide, daisy-like, consisting of drooping, yellow petals surrounding a brown center that appear in July and August.
TEXTURE: Coarse.
CULTURE: Full sun to partial shade. Adapts to any well drained soil. Remove dead flowers to encourage a second blooming later in summer. May need staking.
LANDSCAPE/ GARDEN VALUE: Use as a background plant in sunny perennial and mixed beds and borders. Also looks impressive standing alone in mass plantings. A native plant great for use in wildflower gardens.
HARDINESS: Zones 4–9.
NATIVE HABITAT: North America.

Solidago hybrids
GOLDENROD

DEER ATTRACTION: Rarely.
HABIT: Upright.
SIZE: 2–3' tall, 18–24" wide.
LEAVES: 4–6" long, lance-like, green.
FLOWERS: Small, yellow, 4–6" long, drooping or horizontally held spikes
 appear in July through October.
TEXTURE: Coarse.
CULTURE: Full sun or light shade. Grows in almost any well drained soil.
LANDSCAPE/ GARDEN VALUE: Use in sunny or lightly shaded perennial
 or mixed beds and borders.
HARDINESS: Zones 3–9.
NATIVE HABITAT: North America, Europe, Asia, and South America.
SPECIAL CHARACTERISTICS: Very easy to grow perennial. Many new
 hybrids and cultivars are available.

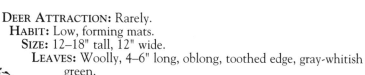

Stachys byzantina
LAMB'S EARS

DEER ATTRACTION: Rarely.
HABIT: Low, forming mats.
SIZE: 12–18" tall, 12" wide.
LEAVES: Woolly, 4–6" long, oblong, toothed edge, gray-whitish
 green.
FLOWERS: 6–8" long purple spikes, appear in late May through June.
TEXTURE: Medium.
CULTURE: Full sun to partial shade. Prefers well drained, somewhat
 moist soils. Not tolerant of dry soils.
LANDSCAPE/ GARDEN VALUE: Use as an edging plant in perennial
 and mixed beds and borders. Also use as a ground cover.
HARDINESS: Zones 4–8.
NATIVE HABITAT: Turkey and Southwestern Asia.
SPECIAL CHARACTERISTICS: Can sometimes look messy as
 stems flop over and lay prostrate later in season.

PERENNIALS

Thymus vulgaris
COMMON THYME

DEER ATTRACTION: Rarely.
HABIT: Very low and spreading.
SIZE: Up to 2" high.
LEAVES: Evergreen, 1/2" long, dark green and very aromatic.
FLOWERS: Small lilac or purple, fragrant, appear on short upright spikes in May.
TEXTURE: Very fine.
CULTURE: Full sun to partial shade. Will adapt to almost any well drained soil.
LANDSCAPE/ GARDEN VALUE: Use in rock gardens or edges of borders. Can be planted and grown between stepping stones and in the cracks and crevices of rock walls.
HARDINESS: Zone 6.
NATIVE HABITAT: Southern Europe.
SPECIAL CHARACTERISTICS: Often used as an herb for flavoring foods.

Tiarella cordifolia
FOAMFLOWER

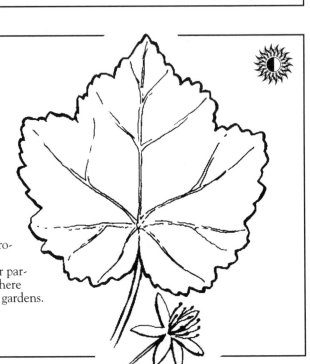

DEER ATTRACTION: Rarely.
HABIT: Low and spreading.
SIZE: 6–12" tall, spreading 18" or more.
LEAVES: Evergreen (in mild climates), 4" wide, heart-shaped with 5–7 lobes, light green and hairy.
FLOWERS: 3–4" long upright spikes covered with small, delicate white flowers. Blooming occurs in April though July.
TEXTURE: Medium.
CULTURE: Prefers partial shade. Does best in organically rich, moist but well drained soil. Will usually spread rapidly if provided with adequate moisture throughout summer.
LANDSCAPE/ GARDEN VALUE: One of the best ground covers for partial shade. Use in perennial and mixed beds and borders where lightly shaded conditions exist. Great for native woodland gardens.
HARDINESS: Zones 3–8.
NATIVE HABITAT: Eastern North America.

Yucca filamentosa
ADAM'S NEEDLE

DEER ATTRACTION: Rarely.
HABIT: Large upright spiked clump.
SIZE: 3–4' tall and wide.
LEAVES: Evergreen, 2 1/2–3' long, 1–2" wide, lance-shaped, stiff and green.
FLOWERS: 2–3" wide, hanging, creamy-white flowers appear on 1–3' tall spikes in July.
TEXTURE: Very coarse.
CULTURE: Full sun. Does best in rich, moist, well drained soils, but is extremely tolerant of hot, dry areas.
LANDSCAPE/ GARDEN VALUE: Use as specimen or focal point in landscapes beds and borders.
HARDINESS: Zone 4.
NATIVE HABITAT: Eastern United States, Mid–Atlantic, southwest to Mexico.
SPECIAL CHARACTERISTICS: Very unique looking, provides a desert or southwest look. Very deer resistant.

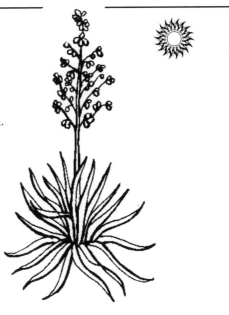

PERENNIALS

Ageratum houstonianum
AGERATUM OR FLOSSFLOWER

DEER ATTRACTION: Seldomly.
HABIT: Low and spreading.
SIZE: 6–18" tall, 12–24" wide.
LEAVES: 1 1/2–3" wide, rounded, heart-shaped, green.
FLOWERS: 1–2" puffy clusters of small blue, white, or pink flowers that cover the entire top of plant.
TEXTURE: Medium.
CULTURE: Full sun to partial shade. Prefers rich, moist, well drained soil with a neutral pH.
LANDSCAPE/ GARDEN VALUE: Use as edging in annual or mixed beds and borders. Good for containers.
HARDINESS: Not frost tolerant.
NATIVE HABITAT: Mexico.
SPECIAL CHARACTERISTICS: Several dwarf varieties are available that grow to no more than 2–4" tall.

Antirrhinum majus
SNAPDRAGON

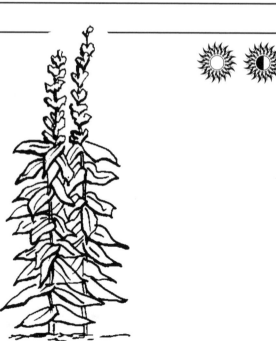

DEER ATTRACTION: Rarely.
HABIT: Upright.
SIZE: 6–36" tall, 10–18" wide.
LEAVES: 3" long, lance-like, green.
FLOWERS: 1 1/2" long, white, pink, red, yellow or orange, appear on 8–12" spikes.
TEXTURE: Medium.
CULTURE: Full sun or partial shade. Prefers rich, moist, well drained soil with a neutral pH.
LANDSCAPE/ GARDEN VALUE: Use in annual and mixed beds and borders.
HARDINESS: Not frost tolerant.
NATIVE HABITAT: Mediterranean region of Europe.

ANNUALS

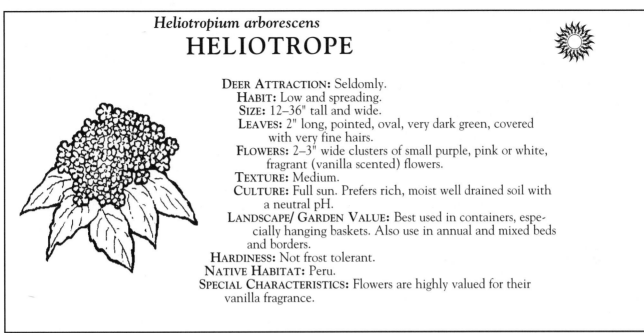

Heliotropium arborescens
HELIOTROPE

DEER ATTRACTION: Seldomly.
HABIT: Low and spreading.
SIZE: 12–36" tall and wide.
LEAVES: 2" long, pointed, oval, very dark green, covered with very fine hairs.
FLOWERS: 2–3" wide clusters of small purple, pink or white, fragrant (vanilla scented) flowers.
TEXTURE: Medium.
CULTURE: Full sun. Prefers rich, moist well drained soil with a neutral pH.
LANDSCAPE/ GARDEN VALUE: Best used in containers, especially hanging baskets. Also use in annual and mixed beds and borders.
HARDINESS: Not frost tolerant.
NATIVE HABITAT: Peru.
SPECIAL CHARACTERISTICS: Flowers are highly valued for their vanilla fragrance.

Ipomoea alba
MOONFLOWER

DEER ATTRACTION: Rarely.
HABIT: Trailing vine.
SIZE: 15' or more.
LEAVES: 2–3" heart-shaped, green.
FLOWERS: 1 1/2–2" wide, white fragrant flowers that open at night.
TEXTURE: Medium.
CULTURE: Full sun. Prefers rich, moist, well drained soil with a neutral pH, but will tolerate dry infertile soils.
LANDSCAPE/ GARDEN VALUE: Use to cover trellis, fences or walls.
HARDINESS: Not frost tolerant.
SPECIAL CHARACTERISTICS: Fragrant night bloomer.

ANNUALS

Ipomoea purpurea
MORNING GLORY

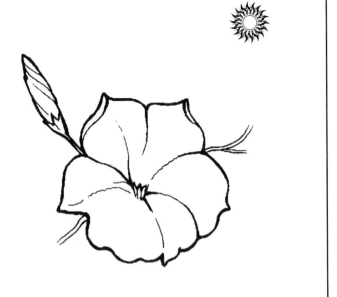

DEER ATTRACTION: Rarely.
HABIT: Twining vine.
SIZE: 15' or more.
LEAVES: 2–3" heart-shaped, green.
FLOWERS: 2–3" wide, trumpet-shaped, come in red, white or purple.
TEXTURE: Medium.
CULTURE: Full sun. Prefers rich, moist well drained soil with a neutral pH.
LANDSCAPE/ GARDEN VALUE: Use to cover trellis, fences or walls.
HARDINESS: Not frost tolerant.
SPECIAL CHARACTERISTICS: Morning Glory can become invasive and is considered a weed in many east coast states.

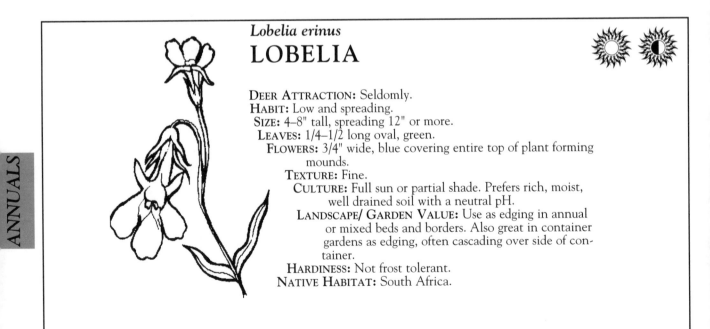

Lobelia erinus
LOBELIA

DEER ATTRACTION: Seldomly.
HABIT: Low and spreading.
SIZE: 4–8" tall, spreading 12" or more.
LEAVES: 1/4–1/2 long oval, green.
FLOWERS: 3/4" wide, blue covering entire top of plant forming mounds.
TEXTURE: Fine.
CULTURE: Full sun or partial shade. Prefers rich, moist, well drained soil with a neutral pH.
LANDSCAPE/ GARDEN VALUE: Use as edging in annual or mixed beds and borders. Also great in container gardens as edging, often cascading over side of container.
HARDINESS: Not frost tolerant.
NATIVE HABITAT: South Africa.

ANNUALS

Mimulus cupreus
MONKEY FLOWER

DEER ATTRACTION: Seldomly.
HABIT: Upright and spreading.
SIZE: 8" tall and wide.
LEAVES: 1 1/4" long, elongated, oval, green.
FLOWERS: 1 1/2" long, tubular yellow flowers with 2 lips and
    spreading lobes that turn orange-brown. June and July is
    the peak bloom time.
TEXTURE: Medium.
CULTURE: Prefers shaded location. Adapts to any rich, moist,
    well drained soil.
LANDSCAPE/ GARDEN VALUE: Use in shady annual and
    mixed beds and borders, especially effective when used
    as edging, in front of taller plants.
HARDINESS: Not frost tolerant.
NATIVE HABITAT: Chile.
SPECIAL CHARACTERISTICS: Great choice for shady areas.

Mirabilis jalapa
FOUR O'CLOCKS

DEER ATTRACTION: Seldomly.
HABIT: Upright.
SIZE: 24–36" tall, 18–24" wide.
LEAVES: 2–2 1/2" long, elongated, heart-like, dark green.
FLOWERS: 1–2" wide, funnel-shaped, white, yellow or red. Flowers open
    about 4 o'clock in the afternoon. Blooms freely throughout the
    summer.
TEXTURE: Medium.
CULTURE: Full sun. Prefer light, well drained soil.
LANDSCAPE/ GARDEN VALUE: Use in annual and mixed beds and bor-
    ders.
HARDINESS: Not frost tolerant.
NATIVE HABITAT: Tropical regions of North and South America.
SPECIAL CHARACTERISTICS: Flowers open after about 4 o'clock in the
    afternoon, a concern if garden or landscape is usually viewed earlier
    in the day.

ANNUALS

Petunia x hybrida
GARDEN PETUNIA

DEER ATTRACTION: Seldomly.
HABIT: Upright and prostrate varieties are available.
SIZE: 6–36" tall and wide.
LEAVES: 1–3" long, pointed, oval, green covered with fine hairs.
FLOWERS: 1–5" wide (varies according to variety), funnel shaped. Many colors available including white, red, purple, violet, and multi colored. Also available in ruffled and double flowering forms. Many hybrids available. Prime blooming time is from June until frost.
TEXTURE: Medium.
CULTURE: Full sun. Does best in rich, well drained soil. Plants may need to be cut back periodically when flowering begins to slow. Pinch back and fertilize to stimulate new blooms.
LANDSCAPE/ GARDEN VALUE: Use in annual and mixed beds and borders. Also great in containers and window boxes.
HARDINESS: Not frost tolerant.
NATIVE HABITAT: Argentina.
SPECIAL CHARACTERISTICS: The availability of many hybrids provides for a great selection of colors, flower, and plant types.

Salvia splendens
SCARLET SAGE

DEER ATTRACTION: Seldomly.
HABIT: Upright.
SIZE: 6–36" tall and wide.
LEAVES: 2 1/2–3 1/2" long, pointed, oval, dark green.
FLOWERS: 6–10" long, spike of small red, pink, purple, or white flowers.
TEXTURE: Medium.
CULTURE: Full sun to light shade. Prefers rich, moist, well drained soils.
LANDSCAPE/ GARDEN VALUE: Use in annual and mixed beds and borders. Also great in containers and window boxes.
HARDINESS: Not frost tolerant.
NATIVE HABITAT: Brazil.
SPECIAL CHARACTERISTICS: Many new hybrids are available.

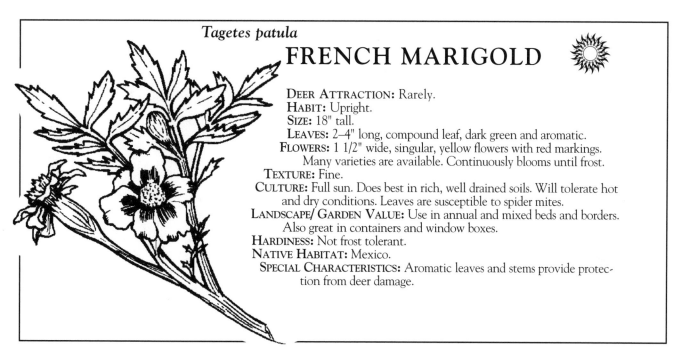

Tagetes patula

FRENCH MARIGOLD

DEER ATTRACTION: Rarely.
HABIT: Upright.
SIZE: 18" tall.
LEAVES: 2–4" long, compound leaf, dark green and aromatic.
FLOWERS: 1 1/2" wide, singular, yellow flowers with red markings. Many varieties are available. Continuously blooms until frost.
TEXTURE: Fine.
CULTURE: Full sun. Does best in rich, well drained soils. Will tolerate hot and dry conditions. Leaves are susceptible to spider mites.
LANDSCAPE/ GARDEN VALUE: Use in annual and mixed beds and borders. Also great in containers and window boxes.
HARDINESS: Not frost tolerant.
NATIVE HABITAT: Mexico.
SPECIAL CHARACTERISTICS: Aromatic leaves and stems provide protection from deer damage.

Tropaeolum majus

NASTURTIUM

DEER ATTRACTION: Rarely.
HABIT: Low and vine-types are available.
SIZE: 12–48" tall, some varieties can spread over 48".
LEAVES: 2" wide, round, light green.
FLOWERS: 2 1/2" wide, funnel-shaped flowers that come in variations of yellow, orange, and red. Single and double flowering varieties are available. Some varieties are very fragrant.
TEXTURE: Medium.
CULTURE: Full sun. Prefers rich, moist, well drained soil. Susceptible to aphids.
LANDSCAPE/ GARDEN VALUE: Use in annual and mixed beds and borders. Also use in containers, especially in hanging baskets and window boxes.
HARDINESS: Not frost tolerant.
NATIVE HABITAT: South and Central America.
SPECIAL CHARACTERISTICS: Leaves and stems have a bitter taste, making it resistant to deer damage.

ANNUALS

Allium giganteum
GIANT ORNAMENTAL ONION

DEER ATTRACTION: Rarely.
HABIT: Arching.
SIZE: 4' tall and wide.
LEAVES: 18–24" long, 2" wide. Shiny, dark green.
FLOWERS: Large, 4–5" wide ball of bright, blue flowers appear on 5' tall stalks in June.
TEXTURE: Coarse.
CULTURE: Full sun. Adapts to almost any moist, well drained soil.
LANDSCAPE/ GARDEN VALUE: Large flowers provide bold interest. Use in a group of 3–5 plants as a focal point in perennial or mixed beds and borders. Also great for accenting shrub beds and mass plantings.
HARDINESS: Zone 5.
NATIVE HABITAT: China.
SPECIAL CHARACTERISTICS: A very unique, colorful, and bold addition to any landscape or garden. Bulbs and plants give off a slightly unpleasant odor.

Fritillaria imperialis
CROWN IMPERIAL

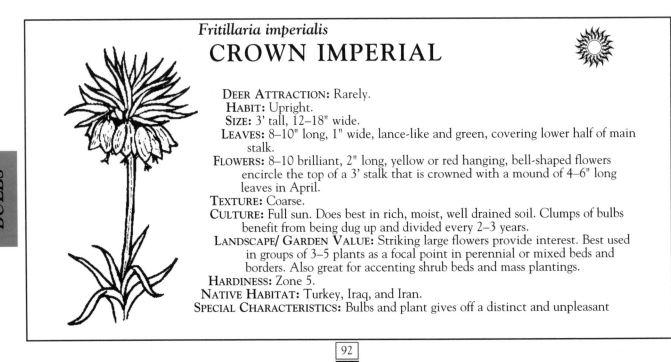

DEER ATTRACTION: Rarely.
HABIT: Upright.
SIZE: 3' tall, 12–18" wide.
LEAVES: 8–10" long, 1" wide, lance-like and green, covering lower half of main stalk.
FLOWERS: 8–10 brilliant, 2" long, yellow or red hanging, bell-shaped flowers encircle the top of a 3' stalk that is crowned with a mound of 4–6" long leaves in April.
TEXTURE: Coarse.
CULTURE: Full sun. Does best in rich, moist, well drained soil. Clumps of bulbs benefit from being dug up and divided every 2–3 years.
LANDSCAPE/ GARDEN VALUE: Striking large flowers provide interest. Best used in groups of 3–5 plants as a focal point in perennial or mixed beds and borders. Also great for accenting shrub beds and mass plantings.
HARDINESS: Zone 5.
NATIVE HABITAT: Turkey, Iraq, and Iran.
SPECIAL CHARACTERISTICS: Bulbs and plant gives off a distinct and unpleasant

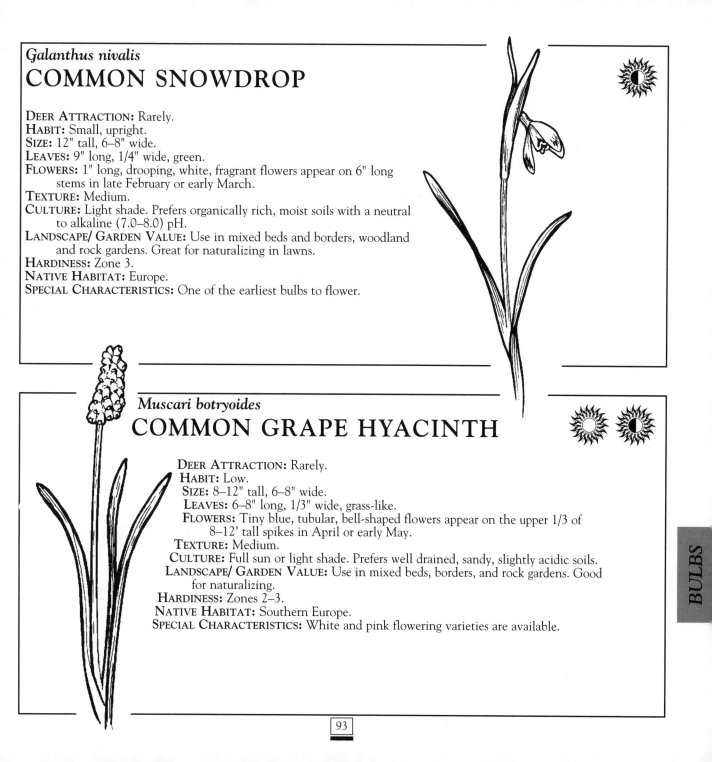

Galanthus nivalis
COMMON SNOWDROP

DEER ATTRACTION: Rarely.
HABIT: Small, upright.
SIZE: 12" tall, 6–8" wide.
LEAVES: 9" long, 1/4" wide, green.
FLOWERS: 1" long, drooping, white, fragrant flowers appear on 6" long stems in late February or early March.
TEXTURE: Medium.
CULTURE: Light shade. Prefers organically rich, moist soils with a neutral to alkaline (7.0–8.0) pH.
LANDSCAPE/ GARDEN VALUE: Use in mixed beds and borders, woodland and rock gardens. Great for naturalizing in lawns.
HARDINESS: Zone 3.
NATIVE HABITAT: Europe.
SPECIAL CHARACTERISTICS: One of the earliest bulbs to flower.

Muscari botryoides
COMMON GRAPE HYACINTH

DEER ATTRACTION: Rarely.
HABIT: Low.
SIZE: 8–12" tall, 6–8" wide.
LEAVES: 6–8" long, 1/3" wide, grass-like.
FLOWERS: Tiny blue, tubular, bell-shaped flowers appear on the upper 1/3 of 8–12' tall spikes in April or early May.
TEXTURE: Medium.
CULTURE: Full sun or light shade. Prefers well drained, sandy, slightly acidic soils.
LANDSCAPE/ GARDEN VALUE: Use in mixed beds, borders, and rock gardens. Good for naturalizing.
HARDINESS: Zones 2–3.
NATIVE HABITAT: Southern Europe.
SPECIAL CHARACTERISTICS: White and pink flowering varieties are available.

BULBS

Narcissus

NARCISSUS, DAFFODIL AND JONQUILS

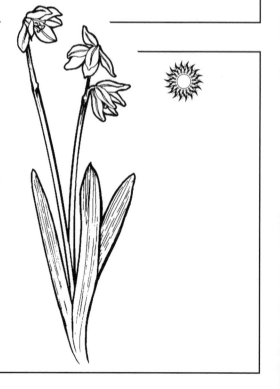

DEER ATTRACTION: Rarely.
HABIT: Upright.
SIZE: Varies according to specie, variety, and cultivar. Some get as tall as 18" or more.
LEAVES: 8–12" or more long, 1/4–3/4" wide, green.
FLOWERS: Vary according to specie, variety, and cultivar. Most common are trumpet shaped, 1/2" to 3" wide and come in yellow, orange, white, pink and various combinations. Blooms late March through May, depending on variety of cultivar.
TEXTURE: Medium.
CULTURE: Full sun to light shade. Almost any well drained soil.
LANDSCAPE/ GARDEN VALUE: Use in mixed beds and borders, woodland, and rock gardens.
HARDINESS: Zone 4.
NATIVE HABITAT: Europe.
SPECIAL CHARACTERISTICS: Bulbs are poisonous to deer and rodents. Most are good for cut flower use.

Scilla siberica

SIBERIAN SQUILL

DEER ATTRACTION: Rarely.
HABIT: Upright.
SIZE: 6" tall and wide.
LEAVES: 6" long, 3/4" wide, green.
FLOWERS: 1/2" wide, hanging deep blue flowers appear on 6" tall, upright stem in late March through April.
TEXTURE: Medium.
CULTURE: Full sun. Prefers organically rich, well drained, slightly acidic soil.
LANDSCAPE/ GARDEN VALUE: Use in mixed beds, borders, and rock gardens.
HARDINESS: Zones 2 -3.
NATIVE HABITAT: Siberia.
SPECIAL CHARACTERISTICS: A white, flowering variety is available.

BULBS

Allium shoenoprasum
CHIVES

DEER ATTRACTION: Rarely.
HABIT: Upright.
SIZE: 8–12" tall.
LEAVES: 6–10" long and tubular, dark green in color.
FLOWERS: Small, 1/2–3/4" wide, rosy-lavender in color appear in
June–September.
TEXTURE: Fine.
CULTURE: Full sun. Will adapt to almost any well drained soil.
Occasionally cut and harvest leaves which emerge from underground
bulblets.
LANDSCAPE/ GARDEN VALUE: Ornamentally used in rock gardens. An essential
in herb gardens. Makes a great potted herb.
HARDINESS: Zones 2–3.
NATIVE HABITAT: Europe and Asia.
SPECIAL CHARACTERISTICS: Mild, onion flavored leaves are used for flavoring sal-
ads and in cooking.

Angelica archangelica
ANGELICA

DEER ATTRACTION: Rarely.
HABIT: Very tall, upright growing herb.
SIZE: 5–8' tall, 3' tall.
LEAVES: 6–10" long, thrice compound, green, very fragrant leaves.
FLOWERS: Large, 4–6" wide clumps of smaller greenish-white flowers appear in late June
through early August.
TEXTURE: Coarse.
CULTURE: Full sun. Prefers rich, moist, well drained soils. Will tolerate dryer soils as
well.
LANDSCAPE/ GARDEN VALUE: Herb gardens. Limited ornamental value.
HARDINESS: Zone 4.
SPECIAL CHARACTERISTICS: Young leaves are used in cooking fish. Blanched stems
may be eaten like celery. Roots and stems are used to flavor liqueurs. Candied
leaves and stems are used to decorate cakes and other sweet foods. Medicinal
uses include treatments for indigestion, anemia, coughs, and colds.

HERBS

Hyssopus officinalis
HYSSOP

DEER ATTRACTION: Rarely.
HABIT: Upright and shrubby.
SIZE: 1 1/2–2' tall and wide.
LEAVES: 1" long, green and aromatic.
FLOWERS: Tiny, blue flowers on 2 1/2–5" long upright spikes appear in July through
    September. Flowers attract butterflies and bees.
TEXTURE: Fine.
CULTURE: Full sun. Almost any well drained soil will do.
LANDSCAPE/ GARDEN VALUE: Herb gardens. Makes a great ground cover or low
    growing hedge. Also makes a great potted herb.
        HARDINESS: Zones 2-3.
           NATIVE HABITAT: Mediterranean.
           SPECIAL CHARACTERISTICS: Medicinal uses include treat-
              ment for colds, flu, bronchitis, bruises, and burns.

Lavandula officinalis
LAVENDER

DEER ATTRACTION: Rarely.
HABIT: Upright.
SIZE: 3' tall, 2' wide.
LEAVES: 4–6" long, very narrow, gray-green and aromatic.
FLOWERS: 4–6" long, spikes of tiny, lavender colored, aromatic flowers that
    appear in June.
TEXTURE: Fine.
CULTURE: Full sun. Adapts well to almost any well drained soil and tolerates
    hot, dry conditions. Cut back to the ground in spring. After blooming,
    prune back to remove dead flowers and rejuvenate plant.
LANDSCAPE/ GARDEN VALUE: Great for use in perennial flower beds and
    borders as well as herb gardens. Can be pruned into a low hedge.
HARDINESS: Zone 5.
NATIVE HABITAT: Southern Europe and Africa.
SPECIAL CHARACTERISTICS: Dried flowers are are used to make fragrant
    sachets. Medicinal uses include treatment for burns, stings, headache,
    coughs, and colds.

HERBS

Marrubium vulgare

HOREHOUND

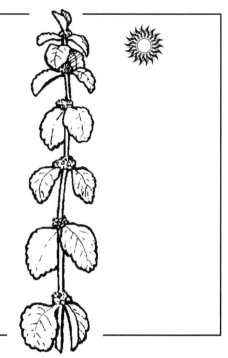

DEER ATTRACTION: Rarely.
HABIT: Upright.
SIZE: 3' tall, 2' wide.
LEAVES: 1 1/2–2" long, almost round with shallow and rounded serrated edges, gray-green in color; hairy. Aromatic.
FLOWERS: Small clusters of tiny, whitish flowers appear along stem where leaves emerge from stem (at axils) in June–August.
TEXTURE: Medium.
CULTURE: Full sun. Does best in well drained soils, tolerates dry soils.
LANDSCAPE/ GARDEN VALUE: Somewhat ornamental, use in herb gardens and perennial beds and borders.
HARDINESS: Zone 3.
NATIVE HABITAT: Europe.
SPECIAL CHARACTERISTICS: Leaves and stems are used to flavor candy and cough drops. Medicinal uses include treatment of respiratory and digestive disorders.

Melissa officinalis

LEMON BALM

DEER ATTRACTION: Rarely.
HABIT: Upright.
SIZE: 24–36" tall, 24" wide.
LEAVES: 1–3" long, arrowhead shaped with serrated edge, green, and aromatic (lemon scented).
FLOWERS: Small white to pink clusters appear where leaves emerge from stem (at leaf axils) in summer.
TEXTURE: Medium.
CULTURE: Full sun or partial shade. Prefers rich, well drained soils.
LANDSCAPE/ GARDEN VALUE: Ornamental use including perennial beds and borders. Herb gardens.
HARDINESS: Zone 4.
NATIVE HABITAT: Europe and Asia.
SPECIAL CHARACTERISTICS: Stems are square (Mint family). Attracts bees. Leaves are used to flavor wines, teas, beer, fish, mushrooms, and soft cheeses. Medicinal uses include treatment for colds, flu, depression, headaches, and indigestion.

HERBS

Mentha piperita
PEPPERMINT

DEER ATTRACTION: Rarely.
HABIT: Upright.
SIZE: 1–3" tall, 2' wide.
LEAVES: 3" long, 1 1/2" wide, pointed, green, with strong aromatic peppermint odor. Square stems.
FLOWERS: 1–3" long, spikes covered with tiny, purple flowers in autumn.
TEXTURE: Medium.
CULTURE: Light shade. Prefers rich, moist, well drained soils.
LANDSCAPE/ GARDEN VALUE: Ornamental use including perennial beds, borders, and herb gardens.
HARDINESS: Zone 3.
NATIVE HABITAT: Europe.
SPECIAL CHARACTERISTICS: Widely used for flavoring foods especially sweets. Medicinal uses include treatment for indigestion and colds.

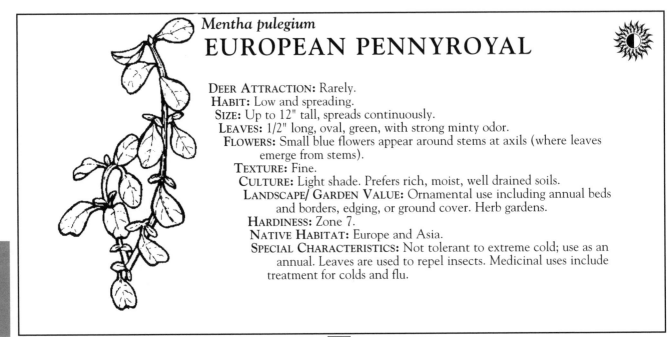

Mentha pulegium
EUROPEAN PENNYROYAL

DEER ATTRACTION: Rarely.
HABIT: Low and spreading.
SIZE: Up to 12" tall, spreads continuously.
LEAVES: 1/2" long, oval, green, with strong minty odor.
FLOWERS: Small blue flowers appear around stems at axils (where leaves emerge from stems).
TEXTURE: Fine.
CULTURE: Light shade. Prefers rich, moist, well drained soils.
LANDSCAPE/ GARDEN VALUE: Ornamental use including annual beds and borders, edging, or ground cover. Herb gardens.
HARDINESS: Zone 7.
NATIVE HABITAT: Europe and Asia.
SPECIAL CHARACTERISTICS: Not tolerant to extreme cold; use as an annual. Leaves are used to repel insects. Medicinal uses include treatment for colds and flu.

HERBS

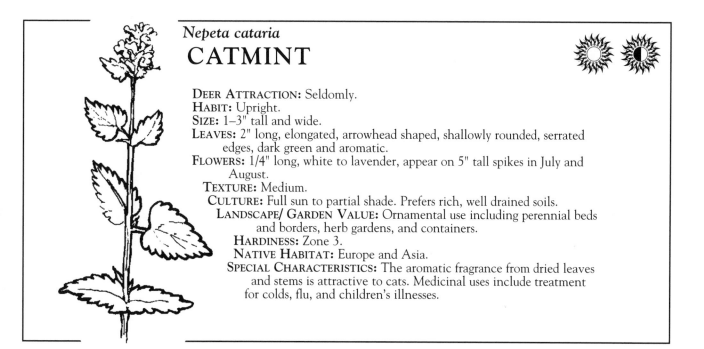

Nepeta cataria
CATMINT

DEER ATTRACTION: Seldomly.
HABIT: Upright.
SIZE: 1–3" tall and wide.
LEAVES: 2" long, elongated, arrowhead shaped, shallowly rounded, serrated edges, dark green and aromatic.
FLOWERS: 1/4" long, white to lavender, appear on 5" tall spikes in July and August.
TEXTURE: Medium.
CULTURE: Full sun to partial shade. Prefers rich, well drained soils.
LANDSCAPE/ GARDEN VALUE: Ornamental use including perennial beds and borders, herb gardens, and containers.
HARDINESS: Zone 3.
NATIVE HABITAT: Europe and Asia.
SPECIAL CHARACTERISTICS: The aromatic fragrance from dried leaves and stems is attractive to cats. Medicinal uses include treatment for colds, flu, and children's illnesses.

Ocimum basilicum
ORIGANUM VULGARE (BASIL)

DEER ATTRACTION: Rarely.
HABIT: Upright
SIZE: 24" tall and wide.
LEAVES: 1 1/2–2" long, pointed, oval, green or purple.
FLOWERS: 1/2" long, white to lavender and appear throughout summer.
TEXTURE: Medium.
CULTURE: Full sun. Prefers rich, well drained soils.
LANDSCAPE/ GARDEN VALUE: Purple and ruffle leaf varieties are great for use in annual borders and beds, herb gardens. Good for containers.
HARDINESS: Not frost tolerant.
NATIVE HABITAT: India.
SPECIAL CHARACTERISTICS: Leaves repel insects. Used primarily in Mediterranean cuisine, most commonly used with tomatoes and for making pesto.

HERBS

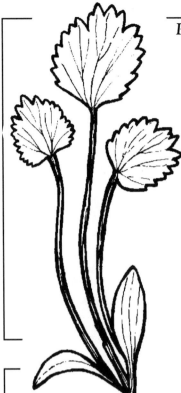

Pimpinalla anisum
ANISE

DEER ATTRACTION: Rarely.
HABIT: Spreading.
SIZE: 24" tall, spreads 36" or more.
LEAVES: 4–6" long, green, deeply notched and aromatic.
FLOWERS: 3–4" heavy clusters of small yellowish-white flowers.
TEXTURE: Fine.
CULTURE: Full sun. Adapts to most any well drained soil. Tolerates hot, dry conditions.
LANDSCAPE/ GARDEN VALUE: Little or no ornamental value. Use in herb gardens.
HARDINESS: Not frost tolerant.
NATIVE HABITAT: Greece to Egypt.
SPECIAL CHARACTERISTICS: Leaves are used for flavoring foods. Seeds are used in curries and in Mediterranean and Chinese cuisine. Oil extract kills insects. Medicinal uses include treatment of indigestion, flatulence, coughs, and colic.

Ruta graveolens
RUE

DEER ATTRACTION: Rarely.
HABIT: Upright and shrubby.
SIZE: 36" tall, 24" wide.
LEAVES: Evergreen, 4–6" long, twice-compound, fragrant and green.
FLOWERS: 1/2" wide, yellow, and appear in July.
TEXTURE: Fine.
CULTURE: Full sun. Adapts to almost any well drained soil.
LANDSCAPE/ GARDEN VALUE: Use as a small shrub. Herb gardens.
HARDINESS: Zone 4.
NATIVE HABITAT: Southern Europe.
SPECIAL CHARACTERISTICS: Medicinal uses include the treatment of strains, sprains, eyestrain, headaches, heart palpitations, indigestion, parasitic worms, insect and snake bites, menstruation, rheumatic and other pains.

Salvia officinalis
SAGE

DEER ATTRACTION: Rarely.
HABIT: Upright.
SIZE: 12–24" tall.
LEAVES: 2" long, oval, wrinkled, and covered with a white fuzz, very aromatic. Most common is green but red, golden, and multicolored varieties are available.
FLOWERS: 3/4" long, purplish-blue spikes appear in June through September. White and red flowering varieties are available.
TEXTURE: Medium.
CULTURE: Full sun. Any well drained soil.
LANDSCAPE/ GARDEN VALUE: Herb gardens, and containers. Varieties with red, golden, and multicolored leaves work well in annual and mixed flower beds as do white and red flowering varieties.
HARDINESS: Zone 3.
NATIVE HABITAT: Mediterranean area.
SPECIAL CHARACTERISTICS: In addition to their ornamental uses, Sage leaves are widely used with cooking pork and poultry and are believed to stimulate digestion. Also known as a healing herb, medicinal uses include treating sore throats, colds, indigestion, hot flashes, and pain. Sage tea is often used as a mouthwash.

Satureja montana
SAVORY

DEER ATTRACTION: Rarely.
HABIT: Upright.
SIZE: 12–16" tall and wide.
LEAVES: 1 1/2" long and narrow, green and aromatic.
FLOWERS: Inconspicuous, tiny purplish-pink flowers appear in summer.
TEXTURE: Fine.
CULTURE: Full sun. Any well drained soil.
LANDSCAPE/ GARDEN VALUE: Mainly herb gardens and containers.
HARDINESS: Zone 5.
NATIVE HABITAT: Europe.
SPECIAL CHARACTERISTICS: Leaves are used as flavoring with vegetables, legumes, and meats such as salami.

HERBS

Acknowledgements

Many thanks to those gardeners who have sought my advice on this subject and encouraged my research into this important horticultural area. Further thanks go to Fred Hicks and the entire Hicks Nurseries Inc. staff, past and present, for their inspiration and encouragement through the years.

Selected References

Curtis, P.D, and M.E.Richmond. 1994. *Reducing Deer Damage to Home Gardens and Landscape Plantings*. Department of Natural Resources, Cornell University, Ithaca, New York 14853.

Jescavage-Bernard, Karen. 1991. *Gardening In Deer Country, Some Ornamental Plants for Eastern Gardens*. Karen Jescavage-Bernard, 529 E. Quaker Bridge Road, Croton-on-the-Hudson, NY 10529.

Sheets, Kathy. 1995. *Oh Deer! How to keep your treasured plants from becoming the main course, Fine Gardening* November/December 1995 No. 46. The Taunton Press, Inc., Newtown, CT 06470-5506.

Ag Information Services–News and Publications. Penn State College of Agricultural Sciences. 106 Ag. Adm., University Park, PA 16802-2602

Cornell Cooperative Extension, Cornell University, Ithaca, NY 14853.

For information in your area contact your state Department of Natural Resources and Environment, Fish, Game and Wildlife or State Cooperative Extension Service.

For Plants and Repellents (including Milorganite)

Hicks Nurseries Inc.
P.O. Box 648
100 Jericho Tpke.
Westbury, NY 11590
(516) 334-0066

INDEX

Latin names appear by plant group starting on page 22. If a Latin name appears below,
the common name is the Latin name.

103

BRICK TOWER PRESS

Traditional Country Life Recipe Series
Biography
Maritime Nonfiction
Historical Fiction
Self-Development
Gardening

MAIL ORDER AND GENERAL INFORMATION
Many of our titles are carried by your local book store or gift and museum shop. If they do not already carry our line please ask them to write us for information.

If you are unable to purchase our titles from your local shop, call or write to us. Our titles are available through mail order. Just send us a check or money order for $9.95 per title with $1.50 postage (shipping is free with 3 or more assorted copies) to the address below or call us Monday through Friday, 9 AM to 5PM, EST. We accept Visa, Mastercard, and American Express cards.

For sales, editorial information, subsidiary rights information or a catalog, please write or phone or e-mail to
Brick Tower Press
1230 Park Avenue
New York, NY 10128, US
Sales: 1-800-68-BRICK
Tel: 212-427-7139 Fax: 212-860-8852
www.BrickTowerPress.com
email: bricktower@aol.com.

For sales in the UK and Europe please contact our distributor,
Gazelle
Falcon House, Queens Square
Lancaster, LA1 1RN, UK
Tel: (01524) 68765 Fax: (01524) 63232
email: gazelle4go@aol.com.

For Australian and New Zealand sales please contact
INT Press Distribution Pyt. Ltd.
386 Mt. Alexander Road
Ascot Vale, VIC 3032, Australia
Tel: 61-3-9326 2416 Fax: 61-3-9326 2413
email: sales@intpress.com.au.